Effective Diversity, Equity, Accessibility, Inclusion, and Anti-Racism Practices for Museums

American Alliance of Museums

The American Alliance of Museums has been bringing museums together since 1906, helping to develop standards and best practices, gathering and sharing knowledge, and providing advocacy on issues of concern to the entire museum community. Representing more than 35,000 individual museum professionals and volunteers, institutions, and corporate partners serving the museum field, the Alliance stands for the broad scope of the museum community.

The American Alliance of Museums' mission is to champion museums and nurture excellence in partnership with its members and allies.

Books published by AAM further the Alliance's mission to make standards and best practices for the broad museum community widely available.

Effective Diversity, Equity, Accessibility, Inclusion, and Anti-Racism Practices for Museums

From the Inside Out

Cecile Shellman

ROWMAN & LITTLEFIELD

Lanham • Boulder • New York • London

Published by Rowman & Littlefield
An imprint of The Rowman & Littlefield Publishing Group, Inc.
4501 Forbes Boulevard, Suite 200, Lanham, Maryland 20706
www.rowman.com

86-90 Paul Street, London EC2A 4NE

British Library Cataloguing in Publication Information Available

Library of Congress Cataloging-in-Publication Data

Names: Shellman, Cecile, author.
Title: Effective diversity, equity, accessibility, inclusion, and
    anti-racism practices for museums : from the inside out / Cecile
    Shellman.
Other titles: Effective DEAI and anti-racism practices for museums
Description: Lanham : Rowman & Littlefield, [2021] | Series: American
    Alliance of Museums | Includes bibliographical references and index.
Identifiers: LCCN 2021042417 (print) | LCCN 2021042418 (ebook) | ISBN
    9781538155998 (cloth) | ISBN 9781538156001 (paperback) | ISBN
    9781538156018 (ebook)
Subjects: LCSH: Museums and minorities—United States. | Museums—Social
    aspects—United States. | Museum visitors—United States. |
    Museums—Employees—United States—Biography. | Shellman, Cecile. |
    African American women—United States—Biography. | Organizational
    change—United States. | Multiculturalism—United States.
Classification: LCC AM11 .S54 2021 (print) | LCC AM11 (ebook) | DDC
    069.1—dc23
LC record available at https://lccn.loc.gov/2021042417
LC ebook record available at https://lccn.loc.gov/2021042418

This book is dedicated to the myriad souls who have left an indelible imprint on the path of my life's journey, and who have encouraged me in great and small ways to share my story for posterity:

To Georges Doll, my high school French teacher, an exacting Belgian whose passion for people, learning, and life sparked a cultural interest in me that continues to this day.

To my family of origin, and especially my parents Victor and Verna, who taught me to strive for excellence and seek truth wherever it is found. They nurtured my love for the arts and indulged my talents. Under their tutelage and encouragement, I learned to read and write at the age of three and have never stopped.

To my dear husband Spencer, from whose love and admiration I derive my strength.

Most importantly, to the many gallery, museum, and arts education professionals I've admired and from whose friendship, wisdom, and example I've benefited, including:

Linda Budd, Ray Halls, Glen Leonard, Tom Putnam, Nina Tisch, Sam Rubin, Esther Kohn, Lisa Menéndez Weidman, Nancy McCoy, Heather Joines Mason, Joyce Baucum, Anicet Mundundu, Kitty Julian, Charlene Foggie-Barnett, Margaret Powell, Laura Lott, Tim Hecox, Aletheia Wittman, Grace Stewart, Ibrahim Shafau, Andrew Plumley, the Facing Change Senior Diversity Fellows, Dr. Johnnetta Betsch Cole.

I thank you and love you from the bottom of my heart.

~

Contents

Acknowledgments

Thank you to my husband, Spencer Shellman, PhD, whose perspicacity, eye for detail, patience, sense of humor, and mad typing skills helped me meet my deadlines.

To Kenshi Westover, who read and advised on specific sections or chapters of my manuscript.

Thank you, Brendan Wiant, for your design support.

I fondly acknowledge my collaboration and cartooning partner, Sam Day, whom I've known since we were teens. Sam's brilliant interpretation and limning of key DEAI concepts that we have discussed have been as helpful as they are hilarious.

Thank you to Beth Zemsky, consultant to the Facing Change Senior Diversity Fellowship at the American Alliance of Museums, whose brilliance and direction in shaping our mentorship of museum professionals in their DEAI work has been transformative.

Finally, I thank the American Alliance of Museums and Rowman & Littlefield for allowing me to express myself through this medium. Thanks for the patience and faith you have placed in me. Charles: Thank you for your encouragement and guidance. I truly could not have done this without you.

~

Introduction

Many museums are strongly reconsidering their practices through the lenses of equity, justice, anti-racism, and pro-Blackness.

The exigencies revealed throughout the year 2020's traumatic realities—a global health pandemic; the national acknowledgment of the crisis of racism in America; the close-to-home trials of job insecurity and loss—have all demonstrated the need in museums for renewed empathy, deep understanding about cultural similarity and difference, acceptance of new perspectives, and radical reprioritizing.

In light of recent events highlighting racial divides and a stark lack of opportunities for BIPOC in the field, museums both public and private must make stronger, more actionable commitments to enacting real change. So many museum practitioners made public and private commitments to learn, change, and redirect their work in meaningful ways, yet the promises remain strikingly unfulfilled. Previous ongoing efforts to address diversity, equity, accessibility, inclusion, and anti-racism have not been incisive enough, nor have they been implemented or agreed to at all levels throughout institutions—from board development to exhibitions to public relations; staff representation and retention; equitable hiring, education, and audience-building; and programming.

Certainly, this is not new: In the last several years, books and articles highlighting museum challenges and calling leaders to action have piqued the interest of practitioners, but many report an inability to transfer what they are reading into actionable steps. As a museum consultant, I have discovered that conveying my lived experience in an environment of professionals who are emotionally prepared to engage in trusting dialogue about cross-cultural difference is critical for building compassion and applying principles to one's own situation successfully.

Effective Diversity, Equity, Accessibility, Inclusion, and Anti-Racism Practices for Museums: From the Inside Out uses personal experiences from my decades-long career as a BIPOC museum employee at various levels and throughout various departments in museums across the United States. As I relate anonymized stories from guests, colleagues, and leaders who navigate their journeys toward a more inclusive and anti-racist approach, I highlight touchpoints that signal moments of concern in the museum, and provide tools for documenting and analyzing similar experiences that may arise in one's own museum practice. The book explores ideas of developing empathy, recognizing behaviors of oppression, problem solving within one's sphere of influence, and bearing responsibility across the institution.

There have been several books on bias reduction in general society, as well as a thoughtful compilation of personal essays specifically about DEAI in museums, published within the last couple of years. This book is markedly different because it uses a first-person narrative, and provides opportunities for museum practitioners to consider scenarios described as life lessons from which they too can draw.

I wrote a book that is part memoir, part business case study compilation, and part workbook, because I wanted to challenge museum professionals to develop a capacity for empathy; recognize their own exclusive or oppressive habits in museum culture or personal comportment; and locate those actions along a continuum of emerging intercultural awareness through a DEAI and justice lens. Activities, exercises, and prompts to chart your own growth toward individual and organizational change will hopefully engender meaningful progress toward long-elusive goals of true diversity, equity, accessibility, and inclusion in our field.

CHAPTER ONE

~

The Only One in the Room

I began my career in the early 1990s in a city and state not known for their ethnic, racial, or religious diversity. I had moved to Utah to continue my education several years before, transferring from an even less diverse and inclusive college in a neighboring state, convinced that the reputation of the studio art program and the university were enough to counterweigh these perceived challenges.

Art school was, in some ways, everything I hoped it would be. The Bachelor of Fine Arts program was intellectually rigorous and demanding, led by brilliant, talented instructors committed to excellence within a nurturing, relatively open environment.

As a young Black woman at that private university, which boasted a student body of thirty thousand, I was part of the 2 percent of African-descended people on campus. I was often, quite literally, the only one in the room who looked like me and shared my cultural concerns. Whether in the darkened art history lecture halls, with the giant filter of light and dust streaming from the back of the room seemingly pointed straight at me, highlighting my difference, or in studios drawing and painting models whose skin, hair, musculature, and gesture were entirely unlike and unfamiliar to mine, I stood out, struggled, and suffered silently lest my discomfort prove a burden or embarrassment to others. I kept my nose to the grindstone and simply did my work.

3

My ambition was to become a self-sustaining fine artist: a painter whose work would be acquired for private collections and eventually museums. At the same time, from as early as my childhood, I had envisioned myself working in the museum field. I admired museum docents. I was attracted to the notion of informal learning. I was taken with the idea of an edifice dedicated to housing and displaying precious cultural artifacts. I remembered how I'd felt in grade school, enthralled by environments that were created to educate and entertain in culturally responsive, engaging ways. My interests in visual art, material culture, architecture, design, public speaking, and human nature led to my infatuation with built environments intended to revere culture and build community.

As a minority in a white-dominated majority environment, I needed to tread carefully. I believed that I had to be as close to perfect as possible so as not to draw undue attention to myself, and I acted accordingly. I excelled in my studies and pursuits not only in the interest of personal satisfaction and as a point of familial pride, but also because the alternative would mean I would prove myself a discredit to my race. It may have been the 1980s in the intermountain West, but it might as well have been the century prior; many of my classmates and some of my professors had never encountered or interacted with Black people before.

To my young mind, I had to be the best example of a Black person that I could be. I refrained from expressing strong emotion. If I raised my voice or allowed my face to reveal an expression of displeasure or anger, I would become the "angry Black woman." I learned to swallow my emotions and school my feelings, at least in public. The last thing I wanted to do was reinforce and reiterate negative stereotypes of people of color that media or imagination had fed my white peers. It was tiring to assimilate, to code-switch, and to cover. For my own protection, I would often retreat. Retreating into my personal world and avoiding intercultural exchange for fear of being ridiculed and marginalized impacted my ability to develop authentic relationships and take pride in my cultural heritage. I buried the richness and symbolism of my African and Caribbean sensibilities in layered poetry, dense prose, and quixotic paintings. After every micro aggression or ignorant, hurtful question about whether I was used to living in trees, or why I "didn't talk like other Black people," I would lose a bit of my shine, sometimes questioning my place, worth, and value.

It didn't help that there were no Black professors: none in my department, and none on the entire campus that I knew of. The campus advisers were predominantly white. There was a multicultural-student organization that hosted regular events. There I met and formed lasting friendships with Native Americans, South and Central Americans, Polynesians, and other international students. It was not a large group, but we depended on each other. My best friends were Brazilian. Our common experience of being minorities in the majority culture and learning to navigate interculturally was the foundation of our relationships.

Graduating from and leaving the university community gave me a freedom that I didn't realize I needed. Shortly after leaving, a dream opportunity materialized.

Breaking Into the Field

It's been nearly thirty years since I started my job as director of a three-story, three thousand-square-foot art gallery in Park City, Utah.

Fresh out of college, having earned a bachelor's degree in fine arts, concentrating in painting, I moved from that college town sixty miles south to a bright, brisk, bustling (at least in the winter) former mining town now famous for the Sundance Film Festival and Robert Redford.

The gallery specialized in two- and three-dimensional work by living Utah artists. An occasional Remington or Gorman made their way to the gallery floor, but by and large the work was by local luminaries from all over the state. Selling paintings and sculptures to collectors, snowbirds, and movie stars was heady, difficult work. I still have occasional dreams at night reminding me of the tasks and troubles of maintaining a robust gallery on Park City's very competitive Main Street, which was lined with other galleries, restaurants, and high-end clothiers.

I largely worked alone, reporting only to the gallery owner, who would visit once a week, working with an occasional assistant, and later managing one part-time employee. I would hire out services that I could not provide, but I would often be the one cultivating talent, hosting receptions and gallery activities, selling, hanging new work, and consulting with artists. Despite its vast difference from the sleepy college town I'd lived in, Park City then and now was not racially or ethnically diverse. Over the years, because of my not being able to successfully fit in culturally and socially, I adapted by excelling at and preferring self-management.

After a few years, I decided I'd had enough of the transactional nature of the art retail business and wanted to try something new. Art had become purely a commodity, and I longed for the educational, interpretive function of arts management.

I got my foot in the door as a museum store supervisor at a bustling, popular museum in the heart of downtown Salt Lake City. Chief among my tasks was to manage two employees and dozens of volunteer (i.e., unpaid) staff who worked on a rotating schedule seven days per week, creating a unified routine with established norms, writing a handbook, and teaching them how to use increasingly more advanced technology (from adding machines to cash registers to point of sale systems).

I didn't miss the slinky catsuit and six-inch heels I used to wear to the fancy Park City gallery or trying to sell as many paintings as I could each month for my salary and commission. I didn't miss driving up and down the slick windy roads of Emigration Canyon during the punishing winters that dumped four hundred inches of snow on us every year.

The museum store was expansive and served as a bookstore, art gallery, and gift shop to locals and visitors. The museum was a popular tourist spot, welcoming national and international visitors every year. That said, there was a marked difference between interpreting and promoting fine art for sale to selling mementos, books, and framed art prints. I was intent on maximizing the potential of my job, emphasizing that museum stores should function as educational hubs for the exhibitions and programming of the institution. Very soon, the museum store began selling facsimiles of interesting primary-source documents and framed prints of original art, art stationery, and other items relative to each exhibit as it was displayed. A wide range of merchandise was developed, at price points and for age levels that were appropriately considered. Collaboration with the Education Department yielded creative and fun ideas. We worked jointly with local and regional vendors to sell corresponding crafts that highlighted the stories of pioneer settlers that we told in the exhibit halls. Soon the store adopted a function critical to the museum's mission and bottom line beyond being a cost center. It enhanced the visitor's interpretive choices for understanding exhibit content. The store became an actual branch of the Education Department, essential to its mission.

Another bright side to the store was that I had found my people: quirky, curious, passionate people with disparate hobbies and encyclopedic memories. There were retired married couples, history- and art-loving young adults, and even a ninety-five-year-old woman who had low vision but who always counted back exact and perfect change to the store patrons. Some of the store volunteers had also trained as docents and would rehearse their presentations during the down hours. The stories we shared, rapport we enjoyed, and commonalities we discovered allowed us to work harmoniously.

I can't remember exactly how it happened, but very soon my colleagues upstairs were calling on me to assist them with exhibition and research projects, and the museum director became convinced that my desires to gain more experience and wisdom as a museum curator could be fulfilled over time in that organization. My opinions and insight were sought and valued. In short order, I was placed on museum exhibit planning teams, then eventually as a team leader in charge of editing and writing museum exhibit text or gallery training guides for docents and educators. I trained the docents on how to conduct exhibit tours for various audiences. Over time, I eventually was given my own junior exhibits to co-curate, and then curate. Our process involved a three- or four-year timeline, requiring of everyone impeccable project-management skills and keen cooperation. Our planning cycles scheduled meetings with the full exhibition team at various points over thirty-six to forty-eight months, so we were planning several exhibitions contemporaneously to be mounted in various galleries in the building. A Phase I plan would entail basic research and gathering data to imagine and realize a full-scale concept over time. Phase VI would incorporate the entire object list: design drawings, installation diagrams and schedule, labels, and mounts. Through this process, I was able to meet and work closely with numerous individuals working across various departments throughout the museum, learning about and supervising their efforts. From the pedestal and vitrine maker to the conservator, registrar, framers, and graphic designers, I would learn so much. Certainly, some of them were skeptical about this *store manager-cum-curator* who was ethnically and culturally different from them in so many ways.

The museum celebrated Utah Mormon pioneer heritage and ancestry, of which I had none. Some of the employees were related to the civic and religious leaders whose portraits lined the halls of the galleries. As with my university experience, several of my coworkers, despite their maturity and worldliness, had never seen a person of color before, especially not a Black person. Coworkers would shyly ask how they should refer to me: Dark? Colored? Was it wrong to say Negro or Black? They were often curious about my upbringing, my experiences in Salt Lake City. As I grew to trust and enjoy the company of my team members, we enjoyed sitting together at lunchtime in the break room or walking across the square to the popular food court where downtown workers convened. It was through this work experience that I learned to trust colleagues and develop a work ethic that depended on others. I'm deeply grateful for caring colleagues, an exacting but empathetic director, and just the right circumstances over the years I worked there that allowed me to leave the museum having written interpretive docent material, curated two exhibitions, co-juried an international art competition, and grown exponentially, both personally and professionally. I often think back with fondness of the fun, the failures, the laughter, quarrels, and joys of just starting out. Yes, I was the only one, as a Black woman—a difference that sometimes made a difference—but the environment and work culture were so affirming and enveloping that I felt it was a home away from home.

When I left to attend graduate school as mature student in Cambridge, Massachusetts, ten years after leaving the university, one of the executives at the museum cheerfully and unironically said I should return to Utah to run the museum someday. This was deeply meaningful, because until that moment, without role models or exemplars from my cultural milieu, I could not imagine leading a significant arts institution; yet, because of the confidence they had reposed in me and the steady mentoring as I learned to be a museum professional, I believed it could one day be the case.

Boston Days

Moving from the West to the East Coast was thrilling and enlightening. I would be nearly two thousand miles away from my parents, siblings, and friends, in a state I had never visited, much less lived in. I'd traveled extensively throughout the United States, but not in New England. I fell immediately in love with the stately European-derived architecture, soft rolling hills, beautifully designed greenspaces, rocky coastline, and blazing, colorful autumns. The Museum Studies program I was about to join at Harvard University's Department of Continuing Education (DCE) was relatively new. It was attractive because it was small, and well worth the sticker price. As with undergraduate school, I had to finance my education without the assistance of loans or grants. It was costly, but I knew that there would be a great return on my investment. I took into account that Boston was a complex and modern city, cosmopolitan and pluralistic, valuing diversity and inclusion.

Imagine my surprise to see that the Museum Studies Program was not as cosmopolitan as I'd imagined. All of the instructors were white. I was one of two Black students in the program—soon to be the only one, as the other woman dropped out of the program shortly afterward—and once again I was faced with course material and assignments that were not consistent with or relevant to my cultural frameworks. I worked two or three jobs during the day and attended school in the evenings. I rarely encountered persons of color, although I again made friends with international students from Turkey, Italy, and South America.

Going back to school in my thirties was humbling but also a positive, difficult, and rewarding experience. In addition to challenging coursework and getting used a new city, there was a technological knowledge gap. The last time I had written term papers, I had written them longhand. I spent hours at the tech lab catching up on computer skills. I worked around the clock and tried to make the best use of my time. My living situations and quality of life were modest, to put it generously. With the high cost of living and unavailability of suitable housing for a single woman, it was particularly difficult to find a place to call home. I would often spend a lot of time walking around the city or visiting museums so as not to return home to my hallway "apartment," or, later, a basement room in a large home inhabited by seven other women, all strangers to me. These additional stressors reminded me of my difference and loneliness.

Much of our museum coursework involved visiting the hallowed museum halls that dotted the region. I took advantage of the relative proximity of New York City, Maine, New Hampshire, and Connecticut. Museums and historic sites abounded in this area. They were expertly staffed, with exemplary exhibitions that I would critique for class assignments and projects. My leisure activities also involved visiting museum spaces. I must have viewed and experienced hundreds of temporary and permanent exhibitions: of delicate glass flowers, fashion, elegant china and cutlery, paintings, sculptures, medieval armor, lighthouses, and cars. Once again, however, the story of nonwhite people was woefully missing. Exhibitions about BIPOC were almost always relegated to culturally specific museums, which were often underfunded and less well advertised or staffed. It was quite concerning. One notable exception was my internship with the John F. Kennedy Presidential Library and Museum, where I led tours and wrote gallery guide materials that referenced and centered the experiences of people of color who lived through the civil rights era. I also credit readings by and about Black stalwarts in the museum field, such as Lonnie Bunch, then a curator and later head of the Chicago History Museum; Dr. Johnnetta Betsch Cole; Dr. Spencer Crewe; and others who had been active for years in the field but about whose prominence and influence I was just becoming aware. I had attended several museum conferences over the years and subscribed to museum-association magazines and newsletters. The few articles I had read that addressed the lack of diversity in museums were memorable and encouraging.

My fascination with museums persisted. After graduation, I moved to New York to become head of education at the Heckscher Museum of Art. I was welcomed into their fold eagerly and jumped into the fray. This was in the summer of 2001. Little did I know that my term there would be short-lived, for reasons that emphasized the need to be attentive to DEAI.

Becoming Introspective

Summer 2001—I remember this day as if it were yesterday: getting to know a colleague outside of my museum on off hours and being peppered with questions. I was shy, and she was querulous about my background and work history. There was a laugh in her voice—not a derisive or sarcastic one necessarily, but a laugh was at once nervous and mirthful. She listed the identity markers and characteristics I had shared with her, saying she had never met someone who looked like me or had come from my background, who had museum-professional ambitions. It sounded accusatory, as though I wasn't supposed to like museums, visit museums, aspire to a museum career. She hadn't encountered anyone like me over the course of her career, so how or why could I exist as a *museum person?*

"Why museums?" she asked repeatedly and incredulously. After some time, I realized she was asking, "Why YOU in museums?" She was asking why I, as a Black woman, a person of color, was so interested in working in, occupying space in, teaching in, and luxuriating in museums that did not seem to reflect the interests and offerings that she assumed I had. Why museums and not a cultural center for the "exotic other?" Why museums and not a plethora of other places that might be instantly more inclusive, or where I wouldn't often be "the only one in the room?"

All of a sudden, memories of the past eleven years flooded back. I thought of the trajectory my early adulthood and career had taken. I recognized my relative privilege in some areas, and how my story somewhat played against type. I had had to claw and scrape for my museum career, but to some degree it was my education, financial independence, and the luck of the draw that initially set me in a direction that signaled possibility. Many other people who looked like me did not start out on similar footing. I began to see how legacy, power, and white privilege informed the direction and interests of so many museum trustees, directors, and staff.

I also realized that there were many more people just like me who desired careers and volunteer opportunities in museums but who were never sought or chosen.

My work on Long Island and time spent in New York helped me to see more starkly the socioeconomic, racial, and ethnic disparities and differences that play out societally, and how they impact access to arts and culture. I saw how critical philanthropy was to shaping the priorities of a museum's reach. Relationships with school districts and higher education are critical for forming partnerships of student access to museum offerings.

When I read, heard, or said that museums were "for all," who was the "all" spoken of? I began to have a critical conversation with myself. I was finally able to see that what I perceived as my unique personal experiences, in terms of race and culture, were amplified and experienced almost universally among communities of people who looked like me, and also impacted those who looked like me who were the "only ones" in their museum rooms.

September 11, 2001

I've always been one to value rhythm, which is probably why museum life has appealed to me so. Whether in a large museum or small, and no matter the type or kind of collection, there's a certain comforting, palliative flow to the day that is beautiful and becoming to those of us who need it.

I was living across a busy street from the Heckscher Museum of Art, where I worked as director of education. In a busy department only a month or two away from the school tour season, my work life was jam-packed, heavy, and chaotic.

That said, it was always so soothing to wake up each morning, tend to my personal routines, dress in my early 2000s pastel power suit, and amble down the lane in the direction of the museum. The breathtaking view would inspire me to hum a tune, or pray, or compose poetry. I would walk a lap or two around the lake until I saw one of the two security guards arrive to open up. I'd sit patiently on the low wall surrounding the administration building, wait until the alarms had been turned off, and make my way into the office building, thanking or offering small talk to the officers on the way.

Then, a murmured set of "mornings," and a clatter of purses, messenger bags, umbrellas, light jackets, and planners followed. Then coffee or tea, with the requisite order-taking—Black, or with cream? How many sugars? Caffeine, or no?—then meetings, work, meetings. I'd slip out for lunch in the city center with one of my favorite colleagues, Marla, at least twice a week. We always ordered the lemon orzo soup, which we swore had "something in it" that reduced us to giggles as we relaxed and got to know each other as good friends. My, that soup was delicious.

The afternoons somehow welcomed the most difficult, challenging, often rewarding meetings: conferences with community partners, outreach to school campuses or community centers, and phone calls with board members, volunteers, teaching artists, portfolio review students, and staff members.

Late afternoon was a reversal of morning. I never seemed to get out of there on time. It was a short walk back to the yellow Cape house where I lived with my landlady/friend. We kept separate residences and lived separate lives, occasionally crossing paths to borrow a cup of sugar, share a cab into the city, or have the occasional dinner together.

September 11 of that year upended my New York museum experience forever. For a few days after the horror of the explosions and the eventual connecting calls to let family and friends know I was okay, after my landlady, Cathy, had been accounted for and returned home, the days seemed to run into each other, with a thick pallor hovering over the landscape I'd once found so beautiful. I hunkered down inside. I cried all the time. I worked from home for several days. I was afraid to handle mail, with the anthrax scare and all. There were too many memorial services and funerals to keep track of.

I left New York shortly thereafter to return to Boston, but soon the rhythms of the city returned. Soon sorrow turned to hope, which relaxed me and gave way to laughter. Soon fear subsided. Time marched on.

Not everything was the same afterward. Security, even in museums, became much more strict. Travel became burdensome, particularly air travel. Some people trusted each other less and treated others with more suspicion. Museum exhibits and programs became more people-centric. I do believe this was when some of the first serious questions about inclusion in the museum field came to bear.

The JFK Presidential Library internship had been so compelling and the staff so dedicated and supportive that it seemed natural to return to the museum after the dramatic events of the fall. I needed nurturing and reassurance. Museums had become my home, so it was simply a matter of choosing. By January of 2002, I was back at the beautiful I. M. Pei–designed building overlooking Dorchester Bay. I was wounded and worried. The enormity of the 9/11 attacks had consumed me and made me fearful of and for humanity. My director, Mr. Tom Putnam, helped to create a position for me that would tap into my strengths, address my disconsolate condition, and use my broken heart to connect to others who were experiencing more crisis and marginalization than I could imagine. I was asked to create a program for Black and Brown students, but in particular for students from the Muslim community, who were facing prejudice and discrimination in the wake of the 9/11 attacks.

Dialogues on Diversity

Using the award-winning documentary by Tonya Lewis Lee, *I Sit Where I Want*, as the basis for a school-day dialogue exchange with groups of students from different communities, the John F. Kennedy Presidential Library invited dozens of schools to participate in a free program intended to foster cross-cultural dialogue and engage in courageous conversation. Partners from the Consensus Building Institute and others served as facilitators, leading participants through a series of case studies, empathy-building activities, roleplaying, and peer sharing. Students from all-white communities interacted with students of color their own age for the first time. The day of dialogues included a bag lunch provided for the students, allowing a communal exchange that included nourishment of mind, heart, and body. Teachers and students alike were deeply moved by the process.

From Dialogues on Diversity to programs that brought and kept children and adults of color in the museum space, my work at the John F. Kennedy Presidential Library and Museum was intensely focused on DEAI concerns, even though I did not consciously consider the equity, access, and inclusion aspects of the acronym. Yet, because of my experiences and my desire to share the benefits of museums and grow the field, DEAI was there.

Given the creative freedom to develop fun, engaging lessons and interactions for high school students and rising college freshmen, I came up with a number of culturally responsive innovative programs.

As another example: I worked in partnership with a local university (within walking distance of the museum) to teach civics and museum-education classes to first-generation immigrant college hopefuls.

Twice a week at approximately 4:00 p.m., I made my way to the beautiful UMass Boston campus overlooking Dorchester Bay on Columbia Point and signed in with the cheerful, energetic staff at the Urban Scholars program. After some basic check-ins and a roll call, I had the students to myself. The semester-long curriculum focused on civics, but in order to make the lessons interesting and relevant, I tried to make connections with their own interests—fashion, hip-hop, current events, entertainment. They tried to teach me about Fiddy Cent while I got them to read and discuss *Animal Farm* by George Orwell. Their homework was to write a "Four Legs Good, Two Legs Bad" rap, or to discuss Mary Quant's contributions and legacy to fashion.

This was no easy task, but I truly loved the work, and it was easy to love the students. These adolescents hailed from all over the globe. Some were European; there were a few Cambodian, Laotian, and Hmong students. African students from the Democratic Republic of Congo, Kenya, Nigeria, and Sudan, and Spanish-speaking Caribbean students rounded out the roster. They were all delightful.

Our classrooms were mostly within the halls of the 1970s UMass buildings, and later in the new addition. Sometimes we would take walks and have our lessons near the sailboats or catch a shuttle to the museum and finish our day there.

One semester I decided to teach them specifically about museums. They enjoyed touring the main exhibits about President Kennedy's life and government service. They were moved by exhibits about segregation and integration and stunned to learn that President Kennedy was felled by an assassin's bullet.

The chronological exhibits of President Kennedy's life at the JFK Presidential Library and Museum are beautifully and theatrically done. Visitors usually leave the exhibits on a solemn, yet hopeful, note. It was clear that a well-done exhibition could have a lasting impact. Museums are about more than text panels and pictures. They are about stories, truthfully and artfully told.

The Urban Scholars of Spring 2004 patterned their own group exhibits after the JFK Library and Museum's displays. They chose engaging civil rights topics about which they felt strongly, such as Ruby Bridges, the Freedom Riders, and Dr. Martin Luther King Jr. I had promised them a gallery with an exhibit opening to which they could invite their families and friends in two months.

They toiled tirelessly on their projects, working through barriers of language, arguments, teen angst, missing deadlines, and even a broken heart or two. They studied hard and found creative ways to share the biographies and historical events with their own flair.

It was a proud evening for everyone when the exhibit was declared open some weeks later. We enjoyed delicious fare by the museum caterers. Administrative staff and leaders from UMass, Urban Scholars, and the JFK Presidential Library attended and viewed the exhibit texts, photographs, and media with interest and pride. The exhibition remained in a prominent hall for at least two weeks. Our Museums in Motion class had helped these students refine their leadership skills, research habits, collaboration strategies, writing, and primary-source-document and archive-mining skills.

Several museum leadership positions later, increasing in responsibility and focus, I committed to championing DEAI efforts in museums as an independent museum consultant. As I have now worked with dozens of museums within and outside the United States, I am convinced that there are clear merits to analyzing the diversity, equity, accessibility, and inclusion of each interaction or situation in the museum environment, as well as to planning more large, measurable activities.

~

CHAPTER TWO

Why DEAI? Why These Terms, and This Acronym?

Diversity, Equity, Accessibility, and Inclusion

Museum work is nothing if not interesting. Speaking of diversity: the array of skillsets, jobs, knowledge bases, experiences, and information necessary to maintain an interesting, successful museum is dizzying. Diversity is about difference. It's about variety. I had the good fortune over time of working within nearly all the departments and at every level of employment I had imagined attaining. From volunteer intern to coordinator, manager to being on the executive team, from worm's-eye to bird's-eye views, I've enjoyed various vistas and vocations. I've handled art, and gently admonished guests with a "Please refrain from touching." I've worked in dusty offices in back rooms, condition checking objects and artifacts as they landed on the loading dock, working as a registrar, and I've registered children signing up for a summer camp. I've hammered nails into the wall ready for installation, and glad-handed donors with brand-new manicures at sophisticated exhibition openings. I've worked for small museums and large, old venerable institutions and new art spaces.

Just as diversity in function makes a difference, so does diversity in cultures and people. One thing was certain during my time spent in museums: Museums are about stories. Whose stories get told? By whom are they told? It was abundantly clear that there was a glaring lack of representation in the field, particularly among the Black and Brown communities.

Over the years, cultural scholars and practitioners alike have had buzz-words and axioms attempting to describe the state of museums and other organizations relative to their lack of ethnic and racial diversity in the United States. Some of these words emphasized goals, or the desired condition: multiculturalism, pluralism, diversity. Other terms favored strategies: culturally responsive education, cultural awareness. This research has grown to include recognition of other marginalized groups, including those individuals and groups representing sexual and gender diversity, those with socioeconomic need, those with disabilities, and people whose primary language is not English.

Whether *de jure* or *de facto*, people of color, and particularly Black people descended from enslaved Africans, were prohibited from laboring alongside their white counterparts, earning a fair wage, fraternizing with their peers, and forming collegial relationships. Where once these work conditions and relationships, or lack thereof, were mandated by law, they have persisted in workplaces that have not legislated desegregation or that benefit greatly from white-dominant culture and from white supremacy.

These attitudes, beliefs, and behaviors are shown in museums in the following ways:

Bias, both unconscious and conscious. *Bias* is a value-neutral term simply meaning *slant.* However, when this slant, or preference, is for individuals based on their immutable traits, the propensity for prejudice increases, allowing for irrational judgments of another's intelligence, capacity, and propensity for success.

I have observed, been on the receiving end of, and applied my own biases at all of the museums at which I've worked over the past decades. Until it is examined, bias often goes unchecked. Bias can show up in numerous ways. It is an insidious, often destructive tendency that favors some at the expense of others, usually on a whim or from unconscious negative association. Left to itself, bias insinuates itself into relationships and interactions, labeling and assigning doubt or fear to people and practices that do not deserve such dishonor or disrespect.

Sometimes bias is expressed when a candidate is being sought for an open position. Given the choice between two equally worthy applicants, a museum hiring manager might prefer a candidate on the basis of looks, the way a name sounds, a more impressive (read: expensive) *alma mater*, or other qualities unrelated to skill. I served on a hiring panel once where one of the candidates was younger than the other, and a person of color. The POC applicant had more experience, more education, and a better résumé than the white candidate. Most of the people on the hiring team—all of them white but myself—used a scoring rubric and tried as hard as they could to be objective about their decisions. A lone hiring manager, who clearly preferred the white candidate, blurted out that the woman of color most likely had a boyfriend, would possibly move across the country and start a family, and therefore should be rendered ineligible for consideration. It was a shocking assertion, undoubtedly arising entirely from imagination. It was a clear example of the need for teamwork in hiring decision making, as well as objective questions, scoring, and documentation.

Given our propensity to harbor bias and to use it to nefarious advantage, what can we do about it? Simply: Face it. Change it.

I was honored to be invited to serve on the Facing Change Working Group of the American Alliance of Museums in 2017, where for six months we worked to develop common definitions to describe what the field was observing about attempts to decolonize and desegregate museums. The working group published a paper called "Facing Change" that called for professionals to examine their biases, beliefs, and amelioration strategies:

- **Every museum professional must do personal work to face unconscious bias.**
- **Unconscious bias** refers to our automatic, often-unspoken beliefs about various social groups. These hidden assumptions—also referred to as implicit or unintentional bias—influence how we judge others' competency. They shape our expectations for human interaction and form the basis of prejudicial actions.
- We *all* have unconscious biases. The urge to evaluate is an innate human response. Social and behavioral scientists note that the "ability to distinguish friend from foe helped early humans survive."[1]

Every museum has significant work to do. Some offenses are blatant and make headlines. Others are subtle yet just as damaging. Two thousand pounds of feathers still weighs a ton.

Some biases are not unconscious. It's important to note that while many museum staff members, executives, and trustees have the best of intentions and are decent, honest people, there are some people who want to maintain the status quo in white-dominant, patriarchal spaces. Few are as bold as to openly wonder, as did a white museum employee during a DEAI workshop with a theater full of peers, "Why should diversity, equity, and inclusion [vis-à-vis race and ethnicity] matter here? This is a white museum!" Hurtful though the question was, especially since it was asked of me, it was a piece of information that helped me to diagnose the readiness of that department and the museum itself for further DEAI work.

Bias can often serve to reinforce stereotypes and foster discrimination. Discriminatory actions in the form of *micro aggressions* regularly occur in museum spaces. These actions are subtle, yet pointed, creating hostile settings for those from marginalized groups. Individuals who are already marginalized in an environment that allows insults, indignities, and backhanded compliments to remain unchecked cannot thrive. When they try to complain or seek redress, they are gaslighted and disbelieved, further marginalizing them to the point of helplessness and despair. Human resource departments in museums, if and where they exist, may serve to protect the institution rather than the employee.

Examples of micro aggressions include: willfully forgetting, mispronouncing, or mocking names, particularly those belonging to people who are in the cultural minority; asking questions such as "What are you?" to people who are non-binary; referring to employees of color as "token hires" or "diversity hires."

During the Facing Change Working Group charrette, we carefully considered which elements of anti-racism, pluralism, and inclusion museums needed to focus on. Of the twenty professionals around the table, gathered in the DC headquarters of the American Alliance of Museums, most us of believed that a commitment to these values should be demonstrated by every museum seeking validation and accreditation. We noted that diversity was a given: it's a fact of life and must be acknowledged and asserted as a valuable characteristic. Equity, rather than equality, is an intentional redistribution of resources toward a meaningful outcome, leveraging the diversity that is inherent. *Accessibility* refers to accommodating those who need to participate but are by themselves not fully able to do so. *Inclusion* is accepting and celebrating everyone as fully and completely as possible, requiring a constant engagement with internal and external constituents.

My own thoughts about these definitions have grown, and I draw on my experiences to analogize and enlarge them so they will have relevance.

Diversity is about representation. It's about delineating what kind of similarity or difference exists in a situation. Furthermore, it informs which differences make a meaningful distinction in a specific context.

Diversity

In my personal and professional journey, I noticed that my formal education environments and my chosen profession were not very diverse when it came to ethnic and racial difference among the student body, leadership, staff, volunteers, and board members. This was critical because those on the margins—myself and others—were apt to hold back, form superficial bonds, and not contribute fully to a dialogue we were unsure included us.

When I started working at the Museum of Church History and Art in Salt Lake City, it was clear that this organization was not diverse as to race and ethnicity, either. However, I started to grow in my confidence and ability because my colleagues were attentive to equity—understanding what I needed to succeed and providing it for me. They made sure I advanced professionally within the organization, given my talents, expertise, interests, and ability to fulfill their organizational goals. They allowed access, making accommodations for me to successfully become an education curator and allowing me to interpret and create materials for the museum store. Finally, they were inclusive: they made sure I knew I was expected to show up and would be welcome as a full and important member of their staff. They showed that I was respected. I was invited to be on curatorial panels. I led teams and curated exhibits. I was complimented for my work and was a valuable colleague and team member.

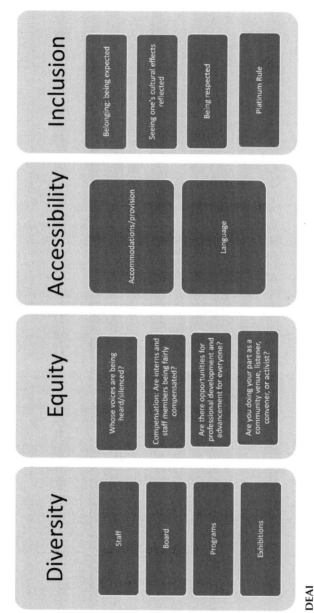

Diversity
- Staff
- Board
- Programs
- Exhibitions

Equity
- Whose voices are being heard/silenced?
- Compensation: Are interns and staff members being fairly compensated?
- Are there opportunities for professional development and advancement for everyone?
- Are you doing your part as a community venue, listener, convener, or activist?

Accessibility
- Accommodations/provision
- Language

Inclusion
- Belonging: being expected
- Seeing one's cultural effects reflected
- Being respected
- Platinum Rule

DEAI
Cecile Shellman Consulting

The museum could have paid greater attention to building diversity in terms of personnel. They did diversify their store offerings, exhibitions, and programs, which helped to attract wider, more involved audiences. However, diversity among staff, volunteers, and executives is continually and critically necessary. It would have been wonderful to share my work and successes with other employees of color, perhaps even mentoring them to build capacity for the field. Having other employees of color in the organization could have prevented the occasional stereotyping, micro aggressions, or communication misunderstanding.

At the time of this writing, I understand that no other Black employees have been hired at that museum in the more than twenty years since I left.

Diversity: More Than Drumming and Dancing

DEAI programs are so new in museums that they are sometimes highly misconstrued. Most people understand the rationale for diversity analytics from an HR perspective as well as the importance of doing business with vendors of varied backgrounds.

Until just a few years ago, diversity planning resided mostly in the area of human resources. If someone asked to see a nonprofit's "diversity plan," this is most likely what would be circulated: tactical goals related to equal-opportunity standards and promises to improve vendor relationships. These aspects of diversity and inclusion are still important to a museum's health and mission because a diverse staff is a vibrant, engaged, and loyal staff.

Community engagement as an inclusion strategy, on the other hand, was an active effort to involve communities that were not, or had not previously been, traditionally included. Special programming would often happen to commemorate certain holidays, or community admission discounts were made available to neighborhoods that were more likely considered unable to pay full price.

I'll raise my hand and admit that February always made me a little nervous. Ah . . . February. Black Month. Bring on the drummers and dancers! Guest performers from Cameroon or Kenya—*n'importe où*—were positioned in public spaces throughout the exhibition halls as a way to somehow pay homage to black history and culture.

Diversity of Thought
Copyright 2020 Sam Day. Used with permission, created for Cecile Shellman Consulting

Yes: I get what they were trying to do—scratch that, what we were trying to do. After all, I was among the museum educators back then trying to find connections between a djembe and a Romare Bearden collage. Sometimes we would tack on an extra fee for the performance or activity. In full "vendor mode," I was happy that we were employing, even for a few days a year, people of color who were highly skilled in their artistic endeavors. It was a good thing to add to the number of Black bodies, faces, smiles, and voices in the museum, wasn't it?

What I didn't count on happening—absent any other contemporaneous efforts to be inclusive—was the sort of compartmentalization that we were initially trying to avoid. Those trained musicians sharing their ancestral heritage became tropes. They were exoticized and, ultimately, minimized since we didn't do a good enough job to do deep research, add content, or just frankly refrain from tokenizing.

When Diversity and Inclusion started to be buzzwords in the field, many museums hearkened back to the "multicultural programming" days for inspiration. While the intent may be pure, there is danger in assuming that "cultural programming" will solve the disconnectedness many museums have with their communities of color, new immigrant communities, and others. In the interest of belonging, we all want to be welcomed and understood, and to feel like we are as capable, intellectually competent, and as valuable as any other visitor. If the museum is going to bring special programs or exhibits in that reflect other communities, the museum should thoughtfully and authentically engage with the community throughout the entire process.

Ultimately, though—as beautiful and rhythmic as the beats may be, diversity and inclusion is not drumming and dancing. It's careful reflection on who is missing from the conversation and why—whose stories are not being told, whose families are not participating in the museum community. What do they actually want to know about, to see in your museum? Have a dynamic dialogue, and go from there.

Equity

Equity is about fairness, but it is more than that. It is the value in the acronym that speaks most about social awareness and social justice. Whereas diversity is quantifiable and refers to enumerating people, objects, and facts, equity is about leveraging similarities and differences to ensure that all concerned have the resources, power, and hope they need to excel in the environment.

Some museum staff will come to the institution well credentialed, with years of experience, valuable contacts, and community ties. Others will possess the skills for which they ostensibly are hired but quickly find that there are hierarchies, inconsistences, and cultural norms that value certain characteristics or traits over others—usually characteristics that the skilled-but-unseasoned newcomer does not possess. These examples of inequity can be subtle: After all, isn't it a good thing to create a common culture based on shared norms and practices? What's wrong with hiring a development director who's "conventionally attractive," a good party thrower, and who has connections to the deepest pockets in town?

To pay attention to equity means to engage and champion voices that have been silenced through law or tradition. It means finding opportunities for such individuals and the objects of their creative practice to flourish. It means examining and rooting out bias when it occurs, especially where it disfavors marginalized people. It means being authentic as an institution committed to justice, and committing as individuals to making necessary changes within oneself and one's sphere of influence.

I can't help thinking back a handful of years to a stunningly bigoted experience in Pittsburgh involving a talented young artist by the name of Alisha Wormsley. She is known for Afro-futurist work with adults and children in the Homewood neighborhood of Pittsburgh, Pennsylvania. Imagine them up to their elbows in bright-colored inks, stenciling and screening a profoundly important phrase onto fabric and paper:

"There are black people in the future."

Ms. Wormsley's work has always been thoughtful and unapologetic. Back in 2011, I was the mentor for and curator of her first solo effort; she was a fellow at the August Wilson Center for African American Culture, where I was artistic director for the visual arts. Her pieces were dramatic and powerful, complex ideologically, but also beautifully simple and easy to access. She incorporated altars, Orishas, movement, and memory into stark statements about the sacred nature of black life.

I have followed her career since then, as she taught art in the city and refined her own process. About a year ago, a poignant project she had once incorporated into a local museum was installed as an outdoor piece, looming over buildings at a busy gentrified city intersection:

There Are Black People in the Future

When I think of or read this phrase, I feel pride and happiness—to know that in the future, I will exist; my words have power, my actions have merit, and they can affect the future.

I was unprepared for the hue and cry that would ensue when the art project was launched in the East Liberty, a newly gentrified section of the city. These seven words, true and unashamed, were deemed "too political" and too incendiary to remain in place. It took legal action, over the course of several days, for the words to be allowed, notwithstanding the art project had a limited life in the first place.

That there was any doubt about the sentiment or the expression of it in public made me weep, then made me fear: "Am I not wanted in the future?" And what about in the present?

Why is the presence of blackness so feared and laden with horror or dread? If the placard had read "There are white people in the future," would what would the reaction have been?

Alisha Wormsley's project has found new life in various places since the first iteration. The phrase was displayed quietly at the local art museum; it was dwarfed by other messages, colors, lines, and shapes. It was included in a vast array of expressions of contemporary and future thoughts in a gallery dedicated to experiments.

Museums are not just walls on which to hang pretty pictures, nor are they visual storage. Every object holds a message—whether a celebration of inclusion, a treatise on the magnificence of light, or memories of forgotten places. There is choice and intention behind the selection of images, where and how they'll be displayed, how prominently and how long they'll be displayed, and with which funds.

If museums are expected to share in the social responsibility to champion justice and anti-oppression, it's imperative that we embrace the bravery of taking a stand.

Or else there'll be no museums in the future.

I'm thankful that many museums are becoming aware of inequity and trying to resolve it. Museum culture is tough, though. It truly is. It's a culture built on pillaging and pandering; on stratification and justification; on legacy, on lust, and on loss.

Museums don't like to be called out on their sins. They like to present the most elegant, tidy treasures on pedestals under gleaming vitrines, as if to say nothing else matters now that there's a three-by-five-inch label exactly at right angles next to the sculpture.

But we all know, and suffer under the knowledge, that there is tremendous wage disparity across job functions; sexism, racism, homophobia and other LGBTQ-unfriendly behavior; and an unwillingness at times to be open in our communications about these problems. After all: the show must go on! Or up!

Fear is the enemy of progress. We fear that if we start talking about inequity, or advocating for what we want, we will be in trouble, or be less highly regarded, or worse.

Some museums have policies that deter employees from speaking up or out. One museum I learned of at a national conference actually punished staff members who convened a reading group about diversity and inclusion.

So how do we face our fears and move forward?

1. Realize that your activism, however limited, is a part of you. It's an outgrowth of your own belief. Nurture, treasure, and use it. Share it.
2. Find allies and like-minded friends or mentors inside and outside your museum. Make new friends, and don't be afraid to let them know where you stand.
3. Complain when needed, but bring workable solutions.
4. If you see something—say something. Know what to report, when to report it, how, and to whom. This will differ depending on the organization.
5. Be the change you want to see. Be brave enough to be an example for others to see and emulate.

Accessibility

To be human, at the most profound level, is to encounter honestly the inescapable circumstances that constrain us yet muster the courage to struggle compassionately for our own unique individualities and for more democratic and free societies.

—Cornel West

Accessibility is about meeting people where they are, anticipating needs, fulfilling those needs, and accommodating requirements in a manner that bespeaks respect. These accommodations can come in the form of Americans with Disabilities Act (ADA)–mandated equipment and support, or it can be to specific to temporary conditions such as pregnancy or recovering from an ailment. Additionally, one can provide accommodations for those who speak languages other than the one spoken by the museum's majority.

Is Your Museum Truly Accessible?

I enjoy perusing museum websites, especially those I'm planning to visit in person. Very often, the style, typography, content, images, and tone of a museum's website hold additional cues about the institution itself.

These cues go beyond artful graphics and creative language. Color combinations, typefaces, translation features, and contrast levels might cue one in to how welcoming the museum might truly be to all people.

I can surmise how professional and attentive a museum's staff might be when I see the attention to detail or colloquial tone the website's writing suggests. I can understand how thoughtful they are if their visitor-services page gives helpful information that allows me to adequately prepare for my visit. For instance, it would be nice to know beforehand if large purses are not allowed in the exhibition halls. I'll know to leave my big bag at home.

For some visitors, the webpage is critical to their future enjoyment of venues like museums. It's not just about what to bring, what to wear, or how much the parking may cost. Visitors who may experience disabilities such as low vision or blindness, deafness or hearing impairment, lack of full mobility, or cognitive impairments may have those issues to consider, too. They need answers to these questions as well:

Where is the nearest curb cut from my bus stop? How far from there, and in what direction, is a ramp?

What kind of doors will I encounter when I reach the entrance?

Is there a good Wi-Fi connection inside the building, so that I can use the accessibility features on my phone, such as my screen reader? Are there tags and descriptions on your website that make the information intelligible to those using technology as their accommodation in the museum?

Are there comfortable seats placed at regular intervals throughout the museum, including within the galleries?

Where there are multiple surfaces on a floor, are the carpet edges trip-hazard free? Are they weatherproofed and rubberized?

Does the museum loan or rent manual wheelchairs for use? Are your counters in public areas (information desks, cafeterias) and private ones (restroom counters) the mandated height, to ensure optimal use by people who need wheelchairs? Even fractions of an inch can make a difference.

Are there clear instructions for how to request an accommodation, such as ASL interpretation?

Are there photographs (with tags and descriptions) on your website of the kinds of accommodations, apparatuses, and equipment you have for public use?

Do your marketing images show people across the spectrum of ability enjoying what your museum has on offer? Are there written descriptions, maps, and other directional assistance that can be accessed on the website?

Of course, the website is just one test of your museum's welcoming stance toward people who experience disability and those who have other barriers to being fully included. The museum experience itself is the best gauge for determining the efficacy of your accessibility programs, processes, or plans.

On the other end of a computer screen or handheld device is an individual eager to participate in what you've advertised as being "for all." If your single nod to accessibility for those who experience disability is a ramp—well, that serves some, but not others. Certainly not all. If you have no supports for non-English speakers, or for those who find the admission fees too steep, you will want to consider creating some.

It should be said here that while "access" and "accessibility" have sometimes only meant access for people with disabilities, newer museum definitions include any barrier to inclusion that must be overcome.

Here is the American Alliance of Museums' most recent definition:

Accessibility. Accessibility is giving equitable access to everyone along the continuum of human ability and experience. Accessibility encompasses the broader meanings of compliance and refers to how organizations make space for the characteristics that each person brings. http://www.aam-us.org

There are many public and private organizations that champion disability justice, serve language learners, provide services to the indigent and elderly, and work with many people who belong to various other communities. Partner with these organizations and with individuals to see how you can best be of help and service to them.

Remember that in the case of making your museum accessible to those with disabilities, it's both the law and the right thing to do. The ADA is merely one of the pieces of legislation that must be followed.

I often bristle when I see a museum advertising that they are "fully accessible." Very few are. Let that be a goal for us all.

Inclusion

Inclusion is about belonging. It's about providing the perfect fit, the way a magnetic connection fits into a port so that energy can be enhanced, transferred, used, and enjoyed for mutual benefit.

Every time I think about "making a museum more welcoming," I imagine the "Be our guest" scene from *Beauty and the Beast*. From Lumière to Mrs. Potts, all the inanimate characters were scrambling about the Beast's mansion, trying to make newcomer Belle feel welcome in her new digs.

This isn't exactly the same thing, but close. Museums, like the Beast's mansion, can seem quaint, hard to navigate, forbidding, confusing, and overwhelming. At the same time, would-be guests are told: "This museum is for you to enjoy! We want you to partake of what we've got to offer!"

If museums are truly for everyone—and if we really mean everyone—here are ten things we could be doing to welcome and include your guests.

1. Have a Visitor Service staff person stationed just inside the entrance, ready to greet and orient visitors. This seems like such a

simple thing, but it can actually help a great deal, especially if your museum, like most, serves multiple purposes and is visited by people with varying abilities. Your admissions desk may not be located in an intuitive, easy-to-identify spot. Maybe there are long lines or crowds, and your visitor just wants to visit the museum store, or visit an office. Perhaps your visitor is blind, has low vision, is of short stature, or otherwise needs assistance to make it to the admissions desk in the first place. Maybe they just don't know what to do in a museum. A friendly face at the immediate entrance would go far to make the first contact with your museum a welcoming one.

2. Make sure your signs are legible, conform to design best practices and accessibility/ADA guidelines, and are consistent with the others. Too often, interior signage is an afterthought and will hinder, instead of help, a museumgoer's experience.

3. The importance of seating in a museum cannot be underscored enough. Museum fatigue is real. Walking for hours on hard marble or concrete is tiring on feet and lower limbs. Try to have comfortable seating scattered throughout the museum.

4. Consider changing any latches, locks, knobs, or buttons that might require fine-motor skills. Replace those with bar handles, larger touch closures, and other disability-friendly apparatuses.

5. Keep a current list of language interpreters or translators—from ASL to Swahili (or whichever languages are most popular in your community, regularly or during a tourist season). See if these interpreters can be kept on call, can teach your staff basic phrases, and can help translate communications if needed.

6. Take special care to keep your common areas obstruction free. Tape down weather floor mats or other kinds of rugs. Don't use sandwich-board signage that could easily topple over. Bear in mind that people who may have visual impairments or cognitive disabilities may rely on consistent, easy to navigate open spaces. Changing those set-ups without warning, or preventing easy flow from room to room is not just annoying; it could be life threatening.

7. Always use inclusive language. Refer to people as they would like to be referred to. Keep "my pronoun is" stickers handy for others to use, and maybe even wear them yourself.

8. Make and communicate policies that preserve the dignity and autonomy of all your visitors and staff. This may mean designating private areas for nursing mothers to express milk or take care of other functions. It may mean creating gender-neutral restrooms.
9. Have food service staffers be aware of issues around allergies, and make sure they are willing to accommodate those with ADA-recognized disabilities such as asthma, diabetes, and living with cancer.
10. Have a suggestion box and email address handy for those who wish to question, complain, or congratulate.

Above all, ensure that your volunteers, staff, executives, trustees, and guests know that they will be emotionally, psychologically, and physically safe in your care and within your walls. Being inclusive should mean that every person understands they are welcome, expected, and respected. Being inclusive is more than checking boxes that relate to solving individual needs. It's engaging in conversation, dialogue, and relationships that authentically communicate what is required for full human participation. It's more than extending a hand of welcome. It's intentionally and freely allowing people to bring their whole selves to the communal table.

So What? Now What?

As I have reflected on my career in museums, I have developed tools to help me coach others in their preparatory work to engage in their own DEAI strategies as well as in developing their museums' organizational plans. I share both my story and these tools with the community to underscore this message: Personal, small-group, and organization-wide reflection is a critical starting point for developing shared dialogue, mutual trust, alignment of purpose, and common terms.

Subsequent chapters will follow suit, continuing with personal stories of museum interactions and realizations. Each story will highlight one or more issues in DEAI practice, challenging the reader to assess their personal and organizational readiness for cultural change and test strategies for implementing new and next practices in their museums.

How Do You Start the Work?

Almost in shorthand, I hear colleagues refer to the arduous, often vexing, matter of DEAI implementation as "the work." However, when asked to enumerate and describe the elements of this labor, most will state a general concept such as "toppling white supremacy" or specific-sounding goals like "help my museum not be so racist." These overarching, aspirational goals, though lofty and admirable, are too vague to be actionable.

Perhaps your goals are from each column in the DEAI table. Maybe your museum needs to diversify its staff as to race or ethnicity. Perhaps there are other areas of difference that will make a difference in how you interact with your internal and external communities. Maybe you're having trouble connecting to the community, especially if you've made a commitment by openly stating your support for Black Lives Matter, but your museum still only collects and exhibits only white artists' work. Do you want to diversify all internal members of your museum community? Know that this can take years to accomplish. You will need to examine the reasons why the state of affairs exists. Certainly, there are factors beyond your control that have existed since the museum was founded, but what other conditions exist?

Decide what you want the work to be, and what your part in the overall approach is likely to entail. After all, it's you and your colleagues who will embark on your particular task. Too often, museum staff members consider "the work" to be a plan that the executive leadership must orchestrate and execute. This work is for everyone, and must be initiated and carried through at an individual and group level. No matter your own identity or culture, or the current composition of your museum with respect to ethnicity or race, you have a unique perspective that is meaningful to the whole. You also have much to learn and unlearn. Whether you have positional power as an organizational leader or referent power as a practitioner interested in social justice and an improved work climate, your voice and experiences matter.

Acknowledge that institutional and structural oppression exist in your museum. Racism, sexism, homophobia, transphobia, and classism are often rife in museum culture, sometimes deeply interwoven into field standards, policy, and practice, and at other times bubbling on the surface in the form of micro aggressions, prejudice, and unchecked bias. Legacy institutions built on colonialism that for centuries have consolidated power and thrived on collecting and interpreting purloined artifacts do not lose their privilege lightly or with ease. Challenging this norm may seem overwhelming. Understand what you have the ability to change now and what will change as a result of cumulative action across the field and as society becomes increasingly enlightened.

Instead of beginning with a checklist of activities for each individual or museum to accomplish to demonstrate their level of competency as fully inclusive, anti-racist, anti-oppressive organizations, I suggest taking a journey that begins at a very familiar starting point: within.

First, it is imperative to define and understand the terms *diversity*, *equity*, *accessibility*, and *inclusion* in the context of social justice in the museum. If the objective is to instill values in the museum and attach action steps to demonstrate those ideals, you will want to be in alignment with those beliefs and actions. If you want to be part of creating a more inclusive work environment that attracts the diversity you seek, you need to accept and practice empathy and cultural competency first.

Taking stock of one's own experience in museums as a practitioner or partaker allows for a more authentic analysis of the inequities and privileges inherent in the museum experience. Viewing the experiences from one's own identity and culture situates the circumstance in self-conversation: "What does this mean to me, and how can I challenge the status quo?" For some people, it may be the first time they are learning about the struggles faced by museum practitioners and museumgoers of color. For others, particularly those who feel the sharp and painful weight of marginalization all too well, it can be helpful for them to name and document their experiences for their own sake and to share with others.

Exercise I: Asking the Right Questions, or Soulful Self-Work

Mapping your personal DEAI journey is beneficial for further understanding how these values are expressed in your own interactions with your community or museum. Here are some questions to consider while working on your self-inventory.

Diversity

1. What are the differences that make a difference in your museum environment? Are you part of one or many dominant groups, or are you representative of one or more minority groups in that space?
2. Do you observe and understand commonalities and differences among employees in your museum?
3. Who is marginalized at your museum or in your workgroup, and in what ways?
4. Who typically benefits from your museum's prominence or success?
5. Do you have the support you need for building, maintaining, or understanding diversity in your museum?
6. Are you emotionally, physically, and psychologically safe as a person in the minority, if you are from a group that is typically marginalized?

Equity

1. Do you consider fairness as a value that applies to the culture of your museum?
2. Do you wittingly or unknowingly uphold inequitable, oppressive structures and practices in the museum within the scope of your reach?
3. If there are individuals or community members in your environment who are from groups that are in crisis, rarely represented, or marginalized, do you have the emotional intelligence, empathy, and cultural competence to bridge differences successfully?
4. Does your museum convene listening sessions and discussions with your internal and external stakeholders to hear challenges voiced by those who need the most support? Do you listen carefully, speak up when needed, and make suggestions? Are you a good ally?
5. Do you connect to others in culturally appropriate ways? What have some of your experiences been in this regard?
6. What kind of power do you have personally and within the organization?

Accessibility

1. Do you know what kinds of accommodations you or others may need to make use of to enjoy the museum as fully as everyone else?

2. What are the barriers to access in your museum?
3. What are some interpersonal or intercultural barriers that prevent full participation?
4. Do you have access to those who can make change in the group or organization? If you are that person, are you emotionally and actually available?

Inclusion

1. Are you emotionally safe at the museum?
2. Are you psychologically safe at the museum?
3. Are you physically safe at the museum?
4. Are you expected to be there? What would happen if you did not show up, or if you were late?
5. Are you respected by your peers and supervisors?
6. Are your interests or aspects of your culture that are meaningful to you reflected in the exhibitions or programs at the museum?
7. Is the environment peaceful or toxic?

Notes

1. https://www.aam-us.org/programs/diversity-equity-accessibility-and-inclusion/facing-change-unconscious-bias-and-personal-work/.

CHAPTER THREE

~

Places of Safety and Refuge

Museums are edifices that lend themselves to quiet contemplation. There's a culture and esthetic of silence, of solemnity and grace. High walls, climate-control features, scrolled embellishments, forbidding architecture—these combine to give an air of remoteness and stature. There are times in my life when, seeking answers to vexing questions, I visited museums to enjoy the beauty around me and know that I could count on having silent moments if I needed them; moments where no one would approach me or talk to me if I didn't want to engage.

I'll admit that it's taken years to feel so comfortable in museums. Even as a single visitor, or a visitor in a pair or small group, I have, in the past, felt observed and judged, as though I did not actually belong.

Marginalized community members pine for that sense of belonging and need to be enveloped in safety. Laws and customs alike send messages, even now in the twenty-first century, that only white-bodied people, or able-bodied people, or straight people, or people belonging to certain religious groups and not others, are welcome to cross the thresholds of the front door and enter a space of entertainment and learning.

No matter how many brochures are sent to museum members featuring smiling preschoolers of various ethnicities and abilities cutting paper doll chains in an art-making day camp, the reality is that would-be visitors are not prone to making regular use of the museum in the same ways that non-marginalized people might, unless intentional, strategic efforts are taken to ensure that safety and trust are preeminent concerns.

Recently, I was leading a group of arts administrators in a discussion about ensuring that BIPOC audiences feel secure and the need for safety in the museums. The question was asked: "What can you do to ensure safety for people of color in museums?" It quickly became clear that there was a lack of understanding about what *safety* actually meant. Many respondents rushed to state that they would never allow any kind of physical brutality or violence toward any patron or staff member at the museum. In fact, some said they would pledge to *increase* the presence of security officers when a crowd of black and brown people was in the museum. It's sad that I feel the need to explain here that this is exactly the opposite of what should be done. Increasing a police presence in the company of museumgoers who happen to be Black, Indigenous, or other people of color for no reason but to monitor them only serves to reinforce negative stereotypes about their propensity to cause harm. It makes racists feel safer and only serves to humiliate people of color.

Yet, time and time again, museums unwittingly create unsafe and unwelcoming environments for adults and children of color, even as they say they are providing outreach and being inclusive.

A couple of years ago, I authored a blog post titled *Why Dante Might Not Want Anything to Do with Museums Again. Ever.* I share it again here to illustrate that notion and to analyze it as a resource.

Why Dante Might Not Want Anything to Do with Museums Again. Ever.

Picture this: a near-perfect spring day, with a stretch of blue sky so hopeful that all the kids lining up for the bus to go to City Art Museum can feel it, too.

Each expresses this in a different way. Some are humming songs they've heard before on the radio, some laughing and chatting and being extra, because it's a special day when they don't have to be in the classroom. Others are unusually quiet, wondering what they did to deserve this uncommon treat. Almost no one at Malcolm Middle School got to go on a field trip anymore.

It used to be that all the third-, seventh-, ninth-, and eleventh-grade kids in the city got to visit the museum. It had been years, though, since a stern superintendent had been put in and the priorities changed. It seemed that all the students ever did now was take test after test. Some teachers thought art class was a waste of time—let alone the museum trip. None of these students had been on a trip to the museum. It had been that long.

The students got on the bus, eagerly sat with their friends, and half listened to the directions by Miss Davis. There were two teachers and four chaperones for the bus of thirty-four Black and Brown students from Malcolm Middle. They'd do the school proud.

The bus snaked up a hill, then turned left and braked noisily. It had only been a half-hour ride, but several of the kids were jostled awake, wiping gound from their eyes or dribble off their cheeks. They laughed and pointed playfully at each other. They were admonished by Miss Davis, who was trying to converse with a uniformed museum representative at the bottom of the bus stairs.

Soon Miss Davis gestured for them to get out of the bus and line up by twos. Noisily, excitedly, the students did as they were told.

Suddenly, a piercing whistle sounded, and the museum rep, whose name was Farley, let out a rapid-fire string of instruction, each starting with the word "No."

If he said "Good morning," Dante certainly didn't hear it. He chuckled to himself, "How rude," as he made his way up the stairs with his classmates. The anticipation had dulled somewhat, but the curiosity remained.

Ten minutes later, standing in the museum gallery, waiting for their docent, the students started to convey their disappointment. So far, the day had consisted of transporting themselves or being transported and standing around. Footmobile to the bus stop. School bus to the school. Coach to the museum. More footmobile. Hardly anyone was explaining anything to them.

The few people with whom they interacted looked almost afraid of them. In fact, everyone they'd seen looked nothing like them. There was maybe one security guard whom they'd seen at a distance who was Black, but nobody else.

Dante was one of the taller kids, and already had a deep bass voice. Sometimes people mistook him for older, and so the expectations were higher. But he was just a thirteen-year-old kid. He was hungry, and annoyed, and still not sure what all of this walking, stopping, and being yelled at had to do with the converging lines he'd learned about in art class.

He wanted to see the Beardens and the Lawrences, and Picasso's *Guernica* if he was lucky. All he had seen so far were glass doors, glass walls, marble floors, and people who stared back at him or quickly looked away. It soon became clear that many of the other museum guests had never seen that many people of color together in one place.

Finally, after about fifteen minutes of walking around and through the building, they could see some colored walls in the distance, behind glass doors. Before entering the gallery, they were given another stern lecture peppered by nos. All Dante could remember later was something about not putting hands on the artwork, and not kicking pedestals. He wondered what a pedestal was, but he knew he was okay because he wasn't planning on kicking or touching anything.

More disappointment. At five-foot-ten, just a couple of inches off his dad's height, he still couldn't see anything. Their docent had just introduced herself and told them to stay in a group where she could lay eyes on them. The problem with this was: with nearly fifty people in their group, only the few in the front could see or hear anything that was going on.

Some students whined and groaned, knowing they'd have an hour and a half yet to endure before lunch on the bus. Despite withering looks from Miss Davis (the chaperones had pretty much checked out), there was some complaining going on. Dante was a little embarrassed for his classmates.

The docent's voice was soft and low. He could barely hear anything, being near the back as one of the tallest, but the things he heard made little sense. He tried to ask questions whenever he sensed a lull in the one-sided conversation, but twice he was yelled at for interrupting. He grew sullen.

Another student (and a great artist), Raeqwon, asked the docent why Van Gogh used all those swirly, thick brush lines. Several of the kids laughed when they heard "Van Gogh." Some of the girls started to dance and sing "Van stop. Van go. Van stop, Van go." The docent looked impatient, then gave a really, really insulting answer that made everyone feel weird and ashamed.

She said something about how the neighborhood they came from had a lot of drugs, and some of their family members, or even the middle school kids were involved in drugs, and Van Gogh painted what people saw when they were on drugs, and could they not relate? Everyone was, like, shocked.

It was a long hour after that, listening to mumbling and never seeing the work of a Black or Brown artist.

The sandwiches and fruit on the bus were a welcome treat.

Three days later, there was a letter from the museum saying that the school children were disruptive and disorderly, and they were not to come back.

This was an actual occurrence with which I'm familiar. The students of that particular school did not return to the museum as long as their principal was still in charge. That museum has very few school groups from communities of color, choosing to focus instead on suburban school districts populated by white children. Some of those districts are also doing away with arts education, and some of those schools serve students with grave economic need. It's highly unfortunate that assumptions about students of color allow exclusionary practices and contribute to feelings of insecurity and unsafety among of BIPOC individuals.

The story of Dante is quite similar to the experiences related by students in Boston on their visit to the Museum of Fine Arts Boston in 2019.[1] I would venture to say that most white-led museums create and maintain similar spaces that are unsafe, unwelcoming, and harmful for students and teachers of color, and then blame those same people for daring to complain.

For those who are similarly nonplussed by this story, here are some specific considerations when preparing a fictionalized Dante and his class for a visit to the museum:

1. Develop a trusting relationship with Dante's teacher, class, and school. Too often, museum outreach and education departments see their potential school groups as clientele, experiments, or numbers to check off or report. Museum educators work very hard and are often the least thanked and compensated of museum professionals. Even so, they should strive to develop pre-visit materials and workshops with new school groups that are slated to visit. Are there museum educators, volunteers, or docents of color? Are they willing and available to come to the schools beforehand as well? Asking

for input and support of POC employees is helpful, but at the same time, do nor put undue emotional, mental, or physical burdens on Black and Brown employees for disingenuous or inauthentic reasons. Develop relations with educators and teachers who want to get together for the good of the students so there will be familiar faces to greet and see in the museum environment on the day of the school's visit. The idea is to create rapport and familiarity with the school group before they arrive. Museum educators can serve as intermediaries between the school and the museum. Perhaps there can be practice sessions, verbal and visual descriptions of the museum campus, drills, games, and other engaging teasers to build excitement. Much of this can occur online, especially in today's coronavirus-informed world. This sort of preparation will build confidence and ownership in Dante's class and teachers, allowing them to approach the museum and its contents with a sense of awareness. It's a matter of safety because, as people of color from a majority-minority school broaching a space that has very few staff or other museumgoers who look like them, the school group will know they also belong, and will be able to maneuver through the physical space well prepared.

2. Fear of Black bodies is an actual phenomenon. In particular, fear of Black men, or groups of Black people, even as benign spectators, is a troubling, well-studied occurrence. The instinctual purse clutching that happens when a Black person enters the elevator, or crossing the street when a Black man approaches, is not relegated to city parks and suburban streets. It's more than the "you're not supposed to be here, are you?" looks that are sometimes given. I think you'd have to see it and experience it to know it.

I have witnessed this when a group of Black and Brown children or adolescents visited a museum. Once it was when a rainstorm pummeled the region for hours, causing the groups that had been scheduled to arrive at intervals to come all at the same time, greeting each other jovially but noisily at the museum's entrance, excited to be there but drenched due to their travels. This particular group didn't happen to arrive in airtight vehicles, parking in the underground garage that allowed guests to enter the museum dry and unperturbed. They were floppy, soaking, and glad to finally be under a roof. They were talking loudly and excitedly. As I made my way from my office down a long corridor to greet them, I saw museum staff and patrons alike scrutinize these guests with a mix of suspicion, anger, frustration, and disdain. At one point, a museum representative spoke to them quite sternly, and it seemed they would not be allowed to enter. They seemed to be causing a commotion, or causing trouble, just by their presence. Would this have happened if they weren't a group of color? I don't think so. No matter the circumstance, no matter the individual—every museum visitor deserves the safety to be treated as though they are wanted, respected, expected in the museum. Groups of Black and Brown children who visit feel that same sense of hostility or incredulity directed at them. Their expressions of excitement or wonder might be said in a deeper voice, using a different timber or cadence, but they're still just kids, having fun, experiencing new surroundings. They aren't in your museum to touch objects or commit any transgressions. They deserve to be allowed the safety of an assumption of innocence.

3. They deserve the safety of being spared racist assumptions. In Dante's class, the docent described Van Gogh's technique as perhaps being attributed to drug usage, and hoped to seek a connection with the students, perhaps ignorantly assuming that those particular children were more familiar with illicit drugs than others. This is more than micro-agressive; it's chilling in its racist overtones.

4. Allow children to be children. Black boys and girls have higher expectations placed on them by white people in terms of comportment and behavior. They are viewed as older, less innocent, and more culpable. They are chided for playful antics that are common to all children.

5. Instead of engaging with Dante's class in culturally appropriate ways, and instead of developing meaningful connections with the class and teachers, the City Museum Education Department punished them by requesting they never visit again. The students had done nothing but be themselves. The message was clear: Black children are not welcome in this museum.

In the fall of 2020, I became aware of a social media campaign called Change the Museum. Anonymous anecdotes chronicling acts of racism,

Cultural Competence is Mandatory
Copyright 2020 Sam Day. Used with permission, created for Cecile Shellman Consulting

sexism, homophobia, transphobia, ableism, ageism, and more proliferated on Instagram and had the museum world watching. Tale after tale of horrifyingly egregious behavior was told.

For many years, museum professionals of color and others who are marginalized in other ways have sat silent, either afraid to reveal stories of similar treatment or too jaded to imagine that their testimonies would be believed.

As pleasant and reputable as the museums I'd worked for had been, there were nights I had returned home in tears, or days I was certain would be my last because I was too depressed to stay. I was angry and aggrieved by comments directed at me and others, some even by leaders in the organization. I've been called the n* word, been mocked about body size and shape, been told, "Nobody is looking at you because you're Black; they're just looking at you because you're fat." Colleagues of color, colleagues who belonged to the LGBTQ community, and others would confide in me stories of aggression and bullying that were actionable beyond doubt, but for the confidences I was expected to keep. Racist symbols scribbled on whiteboards and carved into walls, having Black Lives Matter being compared to Save the Whales; I, too, could fill cyberspace with painful stories of how my colleagues of color and I were never safe from barbs, gibes, hostility, and contempt.

To the inveterate racists and oppressors, I say: Find another profession. Museums are not neutral. They should be places of refuge and solace. They should also be champions of love and justice.

Diversity of community members should bring acceptance, community, and value. It does require intent and action.

What if, deep down, you really don't believe?

The most basic, fundamental principle pertaining to DEAI practice is social justice. Everyone is different. Everyone belongs, no matter their identity, ability, or community. We should value diversity because it is through the interaction with those different from us that we can gain strength and wisdom.

When museums undertake the mammoth challenge of addressing DEAI concerns, it's important to acknowledge that in addition to representing various innate and assumed identities—most of which are immutable—visitors and staff will hold disparate beliefs, be they religious, cultural, familial, personal, or some combination thereof.

We are a sum total of our innate, immutable selves, thoughts, feelings, and beliefs.

If organizational harmony is to be achieved in support of diversity, equity, inclusion, and accessibility, we should:

1. Recognize that in a museum, arts organization, or similar public enterprise, there will be a wide range of beliefs among staff.
2. Not all beliefs should be supported, especially those that denigrate or inflict harm on others.
3. We should strive to Do No Harm, and actively celebrate the differences among us.
4. As an employee, while you are representing and working for an institution that values DEAI, you are required to leave all potentially divisive, hostile, and oppressive language and behavior behind—particularly as it relates to the sacred personal, immutable characteristics of others.

Attributed to Abraham Lincoln, the following quote encapsulates the principle of appropriate behavior.

"My right to swing my fist ends where your nose begins."

Once in a while, a staff member from a museum where I have worked or at which I've consulted short term will ask:

"Must I participate? I have strong negative feelings toward (a certain religious persuasion, nationality, race, gender, etc.)."

I respond in the affirmative: "*Yes.* Your employer has made it clear that for this to work, everyone must participate. One can harbor any number of (odd, or sadly, oppressive, racist, sexist, xenophobic) beliefs in the privacy of one's own home or church, but **at work you must follow the program.**"

Personal and religious beliefs that affirm the dignity of all people and encourage tolerance are always welcome.

The staff member may not even understand or accept that his, her, or their closely held belief and the expression of it in an action or nonaction is oppressive. They may say that it simply conforms to a religious text, or that it is what they grew up believing and they cannot lose those particular beliefs. No matter—they (beliefs and actions) have no place in the work environment and cannot be tolerated if full commitment to DEAI is the end goal.

Examples of these thoughts and beliefs include:

(a) Refusing to accept women as supervisors or equals due to misogynistic ideas about the roles of men and women.

(b) Refusing to acknowledge, accept, or embrace members of the LGBTQ+ community. Homophobic rhetoric still pervades many, but not all, faith communities. Some religions still actively even teach that gay people do not exist. Infuriatingly, these beliefs can translate into emotional and physical harm to LGBTQ+ staff members and visitors.

(c) Being unwilling to work with or around people of different races, whether consciously acknowledging prejudice or not. The underlying persistent belief is that certain races (especially the further they are from white on a color chart) are intellectually inferior and destined to be subordinate. A recent comment by a sports-team owner about Black football players' supposed inability to think intelligently or strategically (brute force, anyone?) is a sad, but common, example of this reprehensible belief.

Intolerant beliefs that become voiced as tenets and develop into hostile actions, including and especially those about white supremacy, must be held in check and ultimately eradicated at the individual level. It's not enough to say that one must behave one way at work and another way at home. People of integrity feel, think, and believe the same from context to context. Racism and beliefs about the supremacy of white people has a way of oozing out and causing obvious, indelible stains.

In February of 2021 Mr. Charles Venable of Newfields, also known as the Indianapolis Museum of Art, presided over a staff that released a job description calling for its core audience to remain white despite their stated commitment to racial and ethnic diversity and inclusion. He was forced to step down.[2] This was not simply an incorrect word choice, a typographical error, or a fluke.

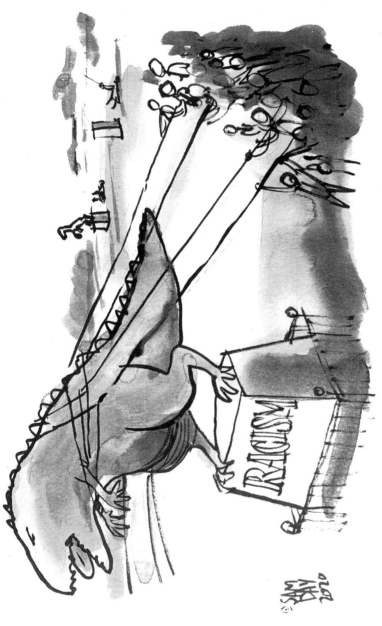

THIS ONE'S GOING TO BE A LITTLE HARDER

This One's Going to Be a Little Harder
Copyright 2020 Sam Day. Used with permission, created for Cecile Shellman Consulting

How many other museums across the United States have similar attitudes about their desired audiences, board membership, visitors, staff, and neighbors: that the white bodies, presence, aesthetic, culture, and sensibilities are preeminent and must be favored and preserved at all costs, even when they eagerly contribute to the erasure and systemic oppression of Black people and culture?

An old biblical saying suggests that "out of the abundance of the heart, the mouth speaketh" (Gospel of St. Luke 6:45). It's critical to observe, log, and deal with all the individual acts of oppression to judge the overall character of the museum. The bile and vitriol will cause a stench that deodorant and breath mints will not cover up. The health of the institution must be worked on from the inside out.

Honor people. Celebrate diversity. Foster tolerance. Embrace inclusion.

Notes

1. https://www.wbur.org/artery/2019/06/25/mfa-racist-incident-students-lawyers-demands

2. https://www.artforum.com/news/charles-venable-steps-down-as-head-of-indianapolis-museum-of-art-85095

CHAPTER FOUR

~

Diversity, Equity, Accessibility, Inclusion, Justice, and Anti-Oppression

I'm always amazed at, and proud of, my fellow museum professionals. These are scholars, dilettantes, amateurs, volunteers, educators, and administrators who share a love for material culture, artistry, theater, education, language, and spectacle.

Often hired at lower salaries than they would earn in other fields, these employees know they must work collaboratively to successfully deliver on their claims. It's a rare museum staffer who researches or creates in isolation.

An example: It's a week before the opening of an important exhibition at a small, but respected, art museum. The building is abuzz with anticipation and energy. Couriers rush specialty labels to exhibition staff. Freight elevators creak and sigh under the weight of grommet-sealed wooden crates. Anxious registrars, clipboards and pencils in hand, calibrate gauges and inspect mitered frame joints. Preparators carefully wheel stretched canvases on dollies across the sealed-off gallery floors and gingerly position them against a freshly painted wall. In the next few days—all hands, all hands will need to be on deck in order for the director's and curator's dreams to come to fruition.

How easily we understand this, up until opening night, when toasts are pronounced, glasses held high in the perfume-and-sweat-scented air, and applause is given. But when the gallery is open, guests depart, and press passes are all given out, where is the hard work and the rejoicing then?

Do we still think well of each other? Do our minds race ahead to the next exhibition project? Do we go back to our too-often striated ways, ranked by degrees and papers published? Do we even remember how to work together?

I have worked in museums that exemplified teamwork, and others that strained at demonstrating basic tenets of respect. There's a near-palpable difference, and nobody's fooled.

When it's all said and done, our memories and relationships will have the most resonance and meaning for us. That condition report or the misspelled name tag, or the rosé instead of the dessert wine will not matter as much as having paid long-standing respect to your retiring colleague, or the one who suddenly passed on.

Why do we do what we do? I hope that in addition to displaying stellar exhibitions and earning a wage, it's to form deep relationships with friends and colleagues: forming community. We need to agree to:

Work hard.
Use things.
Love people.

As museum personnel, we are all just doing our jobs, relying on our skills, and coming together to create exhibits and programs. At one level, fluff and lightheartedness is an important aspect of museum culture. But niceness is not enough.

Museums Are Full of Nice People—Museums Need Professionals Who Advocate for and Practice Justice

Has anyone really worked in a perfect environment? To participate in a shared space, working for a common cause with various personalities at play, is to engage in the risk of relationships that sometimes thrive and at other times fail.

Visit any company review site on the internet or specialty app, and you'll see the gamut—from complimentary love letters to the organization's staff and stewards to scathing, simpering missives that skewer and deride. Some say the truth is somewhere between, but I'm often wont to believe the gut-wrenching words of those who leave, wounded and worn. I often visit potential clients' or employers' review pages on these kinds of sites to see what their outgoing employees have to say about the work climate. Often eschewing or never having been offered exit interviews, employees may turn to the Worldwide Web to offer feedback. One museum whose culture I'm well familiar with received a 2.5 rating, on average, from a popular feedback site. Among the reviews was this stunning claim, in a review titled "Love Museums? Keep Your Distance": "Sadness is the main emotion of staff. Every staff person loathes the institution, so meetings and conversation devolve into complaining almost instantly."

It's from museums like those that I sometimes hear resistance to the idea of beginning a DEAI initiative. The complaint is that resources should be channeled to the employees who are already there; in this case and most others like it, they are the predominantly white employees who are diverse in other ways and whose deeply divisive environs are often the result of poor communication, power hoarding, mistrust, and a lack of emotionally intelligent leadership. The focus on themselves and lack of awareness of civic responsibility to create anti-oppressive spaces also means that any attention to diversifying their staff, volunteers, leaders, and board members will be met with overwhelming resistance—not to mention any talk of equity, accessibility, or inclusion!

Diversity is a bar to clear, for certain, but it's in some ways the lowest bar. Diversity already exists in nature. It may take thought and work to identify which differences make a difference, or which elements of diversity round out a staff, collection, exhibition schedule, or program offering. Infinitely harder is the call to social justice, the exploration of equity, the focus on access, and the never-ending consideration of inclusion. All of these require careful attention, authenticity, and perspicacity.

Diversity as a social justice proposition rather than simply a call to visible representation is, for some, an elusive or confusing concept. For others, it is a moral imperative. At any given museum, there will be some who do not even notice that there are very few people of color, or women, or people with visible disabilities in positions of power and leadership. There will be others who can think of little else, and who arrive at work and leave at night embarrassed and angry that others are not agonizing over the systemic oppressions that maintain the status quo.

I've heard it said recently that diversity should be a concept of the past, with inclusion being the preferred, and more achievable, goal. The idea is that since diversity already exists, there should be, instead, efforts made to leverage that difference and become affirmatively inclusive.

That may be true of some cases and circumstances, but there are many instances and many geographical areas that have not experienced sufficient numbers of people for diversification as to race and ethnicity. At the same time, the aim should not be to represent all heritages or circumstances equally. The aim for diversity needs to be about supporting those who are both least represented and most marginalized in the museum, the field, and society at large. The diversity, or differences that make a difference, in every situation is going to be unique to each situation and organization. If the ultimate goal is to examine what social justice looks like at a personal, organizational, institutional, and systemic level, it's important to take stock of where their particular omissions and inequities lie. At the same time, attention to pro-Black and pro-BIPOC communities means that any serious DEAI effort will consider anti-racism and integration to be key areas of concern. Frank and transparent conversations should occur at all levels and across job functions and strata in order for shared terms and understanding to be conveyed and confirmed. It's one thing to empirically declare that DEAI is now your platform when the organization has not taken the time to convene, coalesce, and consider the risks and rewards of changing their organization's culture, and another thing to accept new people and practices into their inner community.

Museums should be intentionally aware of the need for diversity in order to even consider hiring people of color, people from the LGBTQIA community, and people with disabilities. Museums tend to hire or promote from within, and when outside candidates emerge, there are often the same challenges that plague nonprofits worldwide: How do we ensure that the best candidate pool includes enough members of the communities we claim to desire for our workforce? How can we not just use the same old tactics and expect different results?

If the call to diversity were left to itself, we would see no change in museum recruitment and hiring.

Diversity matters because representation matters. If there are no role models, no examples, no mentors of advancing age, or who are BIPOC, or who use wheelchairs—how will we prove to our youth that it is possible, and that they, too, can achieve?

Museums need to be aware of the unvoiced messages that speak louder than thunder in the echoing marble halls of their interiors. I know of museums that have gone more than a decade without hiring a person of color in a professional position. Does this mean there is no one of color eligible? What does it mean when there aren't even any volunteers of color at the museum?—if there are few, or no, policy makers? Unfortunately, that proves the cynicism of some: that Black and Brown people are just not capable of more elevated jobs, of higher positions, of responsibility and authority over others. In a milieu where repulsion, fear, and ridicule of Black- and Brown-bodied people has reigned supreme for centuries, spoken and unspoken messages will be heard clearly.

Are museums setting themselves up for failure and setting new BIPOC hires up for disaster, ridicule, and psychological ruin when they make facile decisions spurred by peer pressure and injudicious expediency? Should they recruit and hire staff who are culturally dissimilar if they are bent on wresting these eager and talented individuals into forms that cannot contain them and will not be respected by those in control?

High-profile, high-earning positions of implied authority filled quickly by people of color or other visible minorities are signifiers to a clamoring community that This Museum Is Taking Things Seriously. No matter how qualified these candidates are, unless the body politic is sound and serious, united in a commitment to uphold social justice, the venture will fail. The revolving door will hit another exceptional professional on their way out, never truly allowing them a way in, much less having them serve with impact.

Imagine with me a potter selecting and then wedging her clay by hand, taking her time, kneading it firmly, yet lightly, in a familiar routine that mixes and pushes air bubbles out. The type and duration of the handling of the clay depends on its consistency and composition: the potter must know how much grit or slip or grog is characteristic of the type of clay selected. Rolling and mixing the clay is critical. Neglecting to rid the clay of natural lumps and air pockets will mean cracked and broken vessels— wasted efforts—at the time of firing, when the earthenware is forged in a kiln of unimaginable heat.

Do museums truly understand the kind of preparation that is necessary for engaging and leveraging diversity? There's a difference between selecting something from a Sears-Roebuck catalogue and making a conscientious, mature decision to bring new employees, cultures, and strategies into an existing organization.

Maintaining an authentic commitment to social justice is the only way in which equity can truly be at the center of a DEAI initiative. Without that commitment, notions of equality, rather than equity, prevail. Equality is just not possible, museum trustees and executives love to lament, throwing their proverbial hands in the air with a shrug. That is true. There never seems to be enough money to go around (without threatening the exponentially vast bank balances and lives of comfort of senior leaders); there can't be an immediate replacement of the board of trustees with BIPOC and other traditionally underrepresented individuals. Equity is always an upward struggle that must be embarked upon. What are the resources that can be redistributed appropriately? What does *appropriately* even mean, from context to context? Who sets the priorities; who makes decisions; who leads in conversation? Are the ones who typically benefit most making all of the choices, their biases still intact as they preserve and defend their favorable positions?

Emotional intelligence, and particularly, the ability to be empathetic, are essential physiognomies for embarking on accessibility and inclusion efforts. Whether we are talking about disability justice or a broader definition of accessibility, the core idea lies in identifying and anticipating accommodations and needs of those within the reach of the museum. It's attending to the guest's needs, the staffer's requirements, the community member's apprehensions, while ensuring their dignity is kept intact. No person within the influence of the museum should feel embarrassed, put upon, or unwanted for simply requesting what they need to show up as they are in the environment.

What might some of these needs be? The need to be culturally relevant: appreciating and honoring another's culture and comportment enough to tailor choices to suit them to their comfort. It might mean providing accommodations of equipment or sign language interpretation for those who are deaf, or gently cupping the elbow of a blind individual at their request to help them navigate a physical space not visible to them. It might mean creating dedicated spaces for privacy needs; mental,

Privilege
Copyright 2020 Sam Day. Used with permission, created for Cecile Shellman Consulting

emotional, or physical health concerns; or programs for guests who are neurodiverse or atypical.

Inclusion strategies should already be happening at museums that wish to embrace DEAI as a critical measure. These strategies should demonstrate to staff, visitors, and potential visitors that they are, and will be: welcomed, wanted, worthy. A truly inclusive museum will understand that inclusion never ends and is continuous for as long as there are people to be included. For these approaches to truly take hold, every person should commit internally to themselves and externally to each other that they will uphold tenets of dignity and respect toward each other. People should be respected, but not all beliefs are worthy of respect: hate, racism, sexism, anti-LGBTQIA sentiment—those hold no quarter in the community of museum professionals.

Museums must decide on a strategy to engage the work of diversity, equity, access, and inclusion based on their individual challenges and needs. Some museums—especially the ones with already toxic atmospheres—may want to focus on repairing lines of communication and trust before committing at an even deeper level to an approach connected to systemic harms.

Should museums begin by developing a diversity and inclusion office immediately? Should they begin by convening a temporary DEAI task force, or a more centralized, semi-permanent DEAI committee? Should members be paid, to underline a commitment to equity, or should the members be self-selected and unpaid? Do they need to create affinity groups for struggling individuals who have been marginalized by the museum and the larger society?

While answers to these questions are important organizationally, more preliminary questions may be: What is your particular museum like, and what are your needs? Do you know your challenges, concerns, and, yes, problems well enough to determine which strategies to implement and prioritize? Do you know your staff well enough to assess whether they are capable of deep and meaningful cultural change, or will your DEAI initiative merely consist of activities that tackle more performative and public relations-focused matters?

If the objectives are going to take root and have longevity as structural imperatives at the museum, it's critical to situate the DEAI construct at the level where power resides. Unfortunately, that strategy often omits

Community-building

Compliance

Culture

Civic Engagement and Civil Rights

Compassionate Change

Culture at the Center
Cecile Shellman Consulting

staff members and volunteers who are marginalized and most often lack power and authority in the institution, so intentional effort must be made to authentically value and include them in the design, oversight, and implementation of the DEAI strategy and process. Understanding power and its manifestations is essential to the DEAI strategy's success. Who typically gets to make decisions at the museum? Does the museum environment currently support practices that allow others to make meaningful and weighty decisions on their own, without micromanagement, judgment, hostility, and outsized repercussions? Are leaders able to recognize the privilege inherent in their positions, as well as in their whiteness, and are they humble enough to make way for new people and new ideas? Are there open communication pathways that welcome input and innovation from those on every rung of the non-professional and professional ladder?

Personal work and organizational work must happen concurrently and must be extant throughout the life of the individual and institution. Work to remove or control biases; work to become culturally competent and proficient at bridging intercultural differences; work to develop humility, caring, and compassion. These are skills in every way that other skills such as conservation or mount-making are.

The entire museum staff, leadership, directors, and volunteer corps should be involved in surfacing and documenting wrongs and patterns in internal community behavior that cause emotional and mental stress to those in its sphere of influence. Martinet-like behavior on the part of supervisors; disdain for individuals based on class, race, gender expression, or ability; slurs and insults that elsewhere would be written up or even prosecuted outside of the walls of the museum—all of these should be assessed.

Next, written policies, practices, and even budgets should be adjusted to reflect new commitments to a cohesive and respectful environment, as well as one where equity is centered. As far as possible, these commitments should be agreed on as a whole. Perhaps a smaller committee, representative of the entire staff, should write a statement of commitment that definitively states which internal and external communities and identities have been most neglected or harmed by the museum, which communities the museum intends to address or uphold, and what general principles the museum will foster and strive to establish going forward. Despite the temptation, it's important not to reach too high.

- Other-awareness
- Understand culture
- Communicate appropriately
- Work on conflict resolution skills
- Interrupt microaggressions

- Evaluate current practices and consider how the organization is structured; strive for diversity/representation of BIPOC and others who are typically marginalized by museums and other powerful institutions
- Create pathways for those who are typically least represented to have increasingly responsible positions within the organization
- Solicit, receive, and seek to value input about other cultural ideas of organizational structure and behavior
- Work collaboratively to become interculturally competent

- Self-awareness
- Learn about systems of oppression and how one is affected
- Learning about one's own culture and identity
- Understand bias and strive to reduce or eliminate it.
- Understand your own privilege where it occurs

- Understand where, how, and why systemic racism and other forms of oppression affect the museum field and your museum in particular.
- Use your museum's resources and platforms to convene, hold conversation, and strategize with internal and external communities to becoming more civically engaged.
- Commit to the responsibility of being change agents, servant leaders, and shared stewards of community resources.

Start with Self; Work Continuously
Cecile Shellman Consulting

Eager box-checked goals can seem performative, but when you reach too high without checking what's beneath, your slip shows. No one wants a wardrobe malfunction.

If the museum decides to convene work groups, they should be imbued and endowed with official power to make decisions that impact the entire organization. In order for this to happen, an audit of the perceived and actual power within the museum is necessary. There are many kinds of power, and everyone has some kind of power—by virtue of their position, character, personality, and capacity. It is in using this power in trusted relationships that museums can begin to turn a corner in their commitment to DEAI concerns.

CHAPTER FIVE

~

Case Studies and Practical Exercises for Deeper Engagement

Like all complex places of employment, museums can be sites of grace and dignity, yet at the same time harbor pockets of intolerable cruelty and misery. Like the debris that is hurriedly gathered and swept away from the grim corners of the gallery on opening night, these misadventures, once discovered, are quickly brushed aside in favor of the annual report–worthy stories never to be told again in good company, the same way anyone in a well-bred family ought to know that some secrets are just not for public consumption.

As I write this book, some of these cobwebs return with clarity to the front of my consciousness—some egregious, shameful ignominies that happened to me or that I was directly told of or observed, and other situations that happened to confiders who were too ashamed or afraid to report elsewhere.

From the story of the disgruntled museum employee who defecated in the desk that I happened to inherit sometime later; to the supervisor who cried daily in her office, door closed but sobs audible, because her manager was so bent on her own success as to rule with rusty studded iron batogs in each fist; to the racist, sexist, ableist, homophobic, transphobic, and classist behaviors that insinuated themselves into the workplace, perpetuated by employees at every level—in our field it seemed these things went unnoticed or untold. Certainly, they were never dealt with satisfactorily.

Some museums had greater or worse levels of toxicity, of course, at various times or periods of each museum's life cycle. I was privy to some sordid stories the higher I ascended the rungs of responsibility and authority. It was curious that in almost all cases, the people occupying positions at the very top were insulated from judgment, and they could therefore perpetuate that behavior themselves if they so chose, without repercussion. More importantly, bad actors who were positional authorities seemed to argue that they had earned the right to misbehave without consequence, particularly as it came to the treatment of those with less institutional power and privilege.

Sadly, there's almost an unspoken belief that good behavior is an expectation seldom to be pointed out or congratulated—or when laudable acts occur, they should be attributed to the museum itself, not the individual, especially if that individual has little power in the organizational chart. Bad behavior is never completely forgiven, even if it is forgotten. Yet except in hushed whispers, no one talks about these things. In nervous, shocked giggles over drinks, perhaps, someone might say: "That's horrible! Just goes to show it's an old boys' club," and shake her head firmly and disapprovingly. But nothing more would be said on the matter.

This phenomenon was so ossified in museum culture that to air any grievances or differences was to transgress. At the same time, it is abundantly clear that unless we excavate every crevice and corner for behavioral patterns that are harmful and damaging, we cannot responsibly attempt to correct them. We cannot accurately and authentically measure the health of the organization if we don't palpate every lump, thermally image every fracture, and speak to the individual, their family, and their friends about the prescription and path for healing. It requires maturity, bravery, and vulnerability.

Case Studies

I started using anonymous case studies and scenarios a few years ago to describe intolerable situations that might occur in a museum (many of them having occurred to me or others I knew). The exercises arising from the case studies focused on identifying the points of conflict or examples of bias, naming and prioritizing the kinds of problems according to propensity to cause harm to individuals and internal systems, and then recommending strategies to ameliorate the situation going forward, all the while imagining that these situations were occurring in one's own museum work environment. Invariably, clients will recognize similar situations having happened to them, and as a cohort, their privacy about the matter remains intact while we analyze the conjectural one.

When a moment of crisis or concern happens in a museum environment, the impulse to react emotionally, quickly, and punitively is strong. Refusing to reflect on, analyze, discuss, and document situations that challenge our interpersonal or organizational relationship skills will only invite repetition of the same issues and does a deep disservice to others who could ostensibly learn from these examples.

Sometimes it's clear what might need to happen on an organizational or systemic level to change museum practices to become more inclusive. From museum to museum, these checklist items are often the same: Inclusive hiring! Inclusive language! Create a committee! Acquire more representative collections! At the same time, the museum comprises of people, not just practices or assets. These people, to greater or lesser degrees, may exhibit their feelings, thoughts, and beliefs about hierarchy, patriarchy, racism, sexism, anti-LGBTQIA sentiment, and other forms of oppression in subtle but unfortunately effective ways. These behaviors impact the culture of the museum. A reluctant, intolerant, or hostile employee or board member will persist in damaging behavior if these behaviors are not named and challenged. The person who refuses to check privilege or examine bias may refuse to fully execute a directive or follow through with a policy that protects a marginalized staff member or visitor. Some may hide behind their stated right to their own beliefs or claim that, absent a policy mandating equitable treatment, they will not offer such respect to those with whom they disagree or whom they dislike.

Nothing changes if nothing changes, and nothing changes if nobody changes.

We all must modify our damaging behaviors and commit to anti-oppression from this point forward in perpetuity. No matter how beautifully external statements are written by communications teams or the chairperson of the board of trustees, if these behaviors are left to run unchecked, they will remain the rotten core of the institution. When micro aggressions and a panoply of other harmful activities take place, leaders and staff alike should acknowledge and believe that such things are happening. They should convene in small, trusting, respectful groups to discuss the propriety of the behavior and the damage it causes, perhaps in training or workshop situations as well as in staff meetings, and develop or implement policies to ameliorate the situations.

Of course, there will be times when acknowledgment and swift judgment must happen quickly, loudly, and publicly. Make no mistake: these are not the first or only circumstances where such behavior is happening; it is not occurring in isolation.

Case studies are stories recounting interpersonal and organizational challenges at an intimate level. It's necessary to examine and change these behaviors and the root of the issues in order to authentically move forward and outward.

Sharing anonymized, deidentified stories about mishandled interactions or misapplied judgments as a standard practice during meetings and trainings can yield an environment in which humble collective learning experiences can occur without shame or guilt.

Sometimes we tell a shocking story—usually in water-cooler settings as a function of gossip—that we think is clearly indicative of a specific wrongdoing or theme, when the meaning is actually lost on the listener. Once I shared a story of a leader who had pried into my personal life, making assumptions about my dating habits, and then made a wildly racist statement indicating that he believed me to be overly familiar with a number of people. In his words, because "Black people are known to have high libidos." I told my best friend about it. I was angry, embarrassed, dismayed. Her response was to say that the leader should not have said what he thought out loud. I was surprised that my friend did not see the issue as clearly as I did, but instead of dissecting the many inappropriate aspects of this interaction, I kept saying, "It was so wrong." After all, we were talking about exhibit programming! She agreed, but then again, she did not see it in the same way. I eventually left the situation alone, but for years afterward have simmered silently in shame and anger.

How many times do we hear or read about a situation, and then brand the doer of bad deeds with just a descriptive name, be it a racist, a charlatan, a lech, a liar, or a weirdo? But what exactly was the situation, and what do you call the various micro aggressions, prejudices, or kinds of bias that occur? What are the best ways to confront and interrupt those specific interactions in context? How can you create failsafe solutions that will guarantee those situations not recurring in the future? Does reporting help? What are additional considerations?

If you are the one with power or authority in the situation, how do you handle the situation appropriately? What if the power shifts? What if there are cultural misalignments and misunderstandings? Can you identify where the person with less cultural or positional power is contributing to the harm or shirking responsibility, and how would you mitigate any harms or prevent them from occurring it you could?

Analyzing case studies is a powerful process that refines skills of dispassionate analysis and sharpens communication tools. We learn by doing, and sometimes we need practice before going out on the field and connecting the bat with the ball.

Here are ten case studies describing situations that combine matters of diversity, equity, accessibility, inclusion, justice, and museum professional practice. Each case study, or scenario, will be accompanied by questions that allow you to consider the situations from various viewpoints.

I challenge you to make use of these case studies, and then write your own scenarios based on events in your own museum life that you may be ignoring or viewing uncritically or that you might be considering as "par for the course" in museum culture, even though it's actually as shocking as some of the stories I will allude to here. Talk about these situations in staff meetings, DEAI committee meetings, and ethics committee convenings. Using different names and changing details where necessary will remove the temptation to name or shame individuals. Exploring concepts and practicing how to fix certain challenges is the key, not castigating those who may be involved.

When we can see the inequitable practices that are taking root in an organization and how those practices are affecting employees and visitors alike, we can examine policies and procedures that might currently exist to alleviate offensive behavior. If no policies exist, examining scenarios might allow you to ask pertinent next-stage questions about why these practices might be allowed to go unchecked, who a lack of policy might be intended to protect, or whether the lack of policy is a genuine oversight or tradition that fell by the wayside.

Points to Ponder as You Consider These Cases

1. Separate who you think is right from what is right. Your affinity, and perhaps even bias, for certain characters in these stories may prompt feelings of defensiveness, or you may miss the essence of the case entirely. Note that this may be true in real life as well.

2. Begin with the end in mind. Remember that in order to change museum culture, and to achieve the ultimate goal of museums becoming equitable and anti-oppressive spaces, we must view contentious or problematic interactions with that priority as a core value.

3. Remember that although these are highly anonymized, somewhat fictionalized stories, situations like these do actually happen in museums and other places of employment on a daily basis. Refusing to believe recountings of harassment is also harassment. Gaslighting happens far too often at museums. Through these case studies, practice reading about, hearing, and understanding situations that might make you uncomfortable. Sit with that discomfort. Then think creatively, realistically, and compassionately in order to develop new patterns of thinking and, ultimately, practices to replace those that might be perpetuating poor behavior in your own environment.

4. Take every opportunity to practice putting yourself in someone else's shoes. Practice compassion as well as empathy. The goal of convening to deconstruct and discuss stories should not be to castigate, punish, sow discord, or shame others. I believe we can teach gently, model positive behaviors, and continue on a collective journey forged by trust, respect, and hope. Aim to call in instead of calling out. If you engage with these case studies as a group effort in a workshop or staff meeting, make sure not to point out singular failures that will embarrass, accuse, or disgrace individuals, especially in public. Not all egregious behavior comes from malintent. Sometimes it happens because an individual ignorantly practices it, and the culture ignores, affirms, or sustains it.

Scenario 1

Josie is the chair of the DEAI Committee at the Museum of Arts and Culture for All (MACA). This newly formed committee has been charged with making changes in meaningful ways to the policies and procedures governing intersections and interactions throughout the museum and the surrounding community, although there is no formalized process integrating it into the organizational structure.

There are many competing priorities, and this volunteer committee has lost four members (all POC) to layoffs or furloughs as the coronavirus rages on. They are frustrated that they are not making much progress, even though they are meeting to share resources, engage in conversation, and identify areas for improvement. They even wrote a statement decrying injustice after George Floyd was murdered. Josie was not happy when the communications director changed "murdered" to "killed" on the official press release, but she was proud that the museum was one of the first to share a list of promises to the Black community.

There are only four BIPOC employees on a staff of fifty at the museum, three of them identifying as Black. The museum director often talks about inclusivity and insists that showing each other dignity and respect will solve any interpersonal or organizational challenges.

Early in the fall, when staff members were returning to work, one of the Black employees, Dennis, brought with him a stack of Black Lives Matter posters and proceeded to hang them in the lunchroom, break rooms, museum staff rooms, and in hallway near the café used by visitors and staff.

Josie reached out to Dennis in an email thanking him for providing these posters and showing solidarity. She told him she would love to have him on the committee when there was room, but right now the group was too large. In actuality, with four people having vacated the group there was room, but Dennis was not known to be a people person; some found him surly and hostile.

Not long after her email was sent, Josie received a call from the director's executive assistant asking her to schedule a meeting at once. Rumor had it that the DEAI committee had put the posters up, and they needed to come down at once because they were deemed too political.

Please respond to this case study from your own frameworks and understanding, acknowledging what comes up for you as primary issues of concern or insight.

Additional Questions to Consider

1. Why are DEAI committees and task forces often powerless in terms of actionable, accountable endeavors?
2. Does the scenario give any clues as to how or why Josie might have been selected to lead the committee? How important is understanding the organization's diversity profile and needs in determining DEAI resource or governance models?
3. Not being an official member of the committee, did Dennis have the right to bring his own posters to the museum and mount them in public areas? Does the museum—as an organization and as individual people—understand what this action might mean to Dennis and others, including allies?
4. How important is it for people who are marginalized to process, protest, and pontificate about current events that affect them deeply as the events unfold in real time? Does the organization give time, space, and attention to those who are most vulnerable, especially in white-dominant spaces?
5. Does your museum have similar situations occurring, and how are you managing the situations as they arise?

Scenario 2

Briony was the deputy director of a midsized museum in a popular arts city. The museum had an outstanding reputation as a leading authority on early American art, even though the Americans featured were primarily male and white. Briony understood and agreed with the push for collections to be more representative of the community and nation. After all, she had been a chief curator at the institution, researching, recommending, collecting, and exhibiting the works of art over a number of years, leading her team of curators and conservators and working with educators to build the museum's reputation. She was eager to lead the charge in these efforts.

At the same time, Briony was mindful of the lack of diversity among the staff. In her studies and travels, she had met and befriended a number of scholars from across the world. She had enticed some of them to visit as grant-funded researchers or guest curators, but there really weren't any job opportunities for international scholars or curators of color specializing in Native American, Asian, Latin@ or African American art. It was well known that, stacked credential for credential, BIPOC curators simply lacked the heft to fare well as full curators in this highly competitive track. One only had to look at the art history, art studio, anthropology, and museum studies programs to note that there didn't seem to be much interest there.

If Briony were honest with herself, she would also admit that she didn't quite buy this movement to be woke, or politically correct. It seemed forced and artificial. There were plenty of other challenges to worry about at the museum, and funding spent on recruitment of people who traditionally did not show interest in the field or on training for staff to be indoctrinated to be woke warriors could be better spent on already strapped budgets at every departmental level. The existing staff—even though they were white and not diverse in terms of ethnicity, race, or nationality—were intelligent enough and capable enough to curate and collect art by nonwhite, non-male Americans.

Yet, in every meeting with the whole staff, senior staff, or board of trustees, Briony had to make motions to assert that she was fully on board with being more inclusive in terms of staffing. It would mean more mentoring, more time devoted to position creation, hiring headaches, talent management, partnerships with cultural communities, and ultimately more money spent on staff who were not at that point even involved with the museum. Briony would smile and nod when asked whether the staff and museum was ready for the changes that would need to occur to make this situation a reality.

Back in her office, however, she would sulk, stew, and simmer over the institution's lack of understanding of how difficult this was going to be. That said, she needed to remain employed for the foreseeable future; she was only eight years from retirement. She could not afford to make waves or disagree with the executive team or the trustees.

Please respond to this case study from your own frameworks and understanding, acknowledging what comes up for you as primary issues of concern or insight.

Additional Questions to Consider

1. When a museum has a new imperative to be initiated, how are expectations about fealty to that new initiative communicated?
2. How is buy-in determined and secured at your museum when it comes to DEAI matters? Do you assume that all volunteers, staff, executives, and trustees believe equally in and agree to the values you are beginning to identify and espouse?
3. If a staff member has a personal objection to matters of social justice at the museum, how are those feelings, thoughts, and beliefs handled? What's accepted at your museum?
4. Have you considered having your museum make DEAI accountability efforts as competencies by which all staff will be judged, such as in their annual review process?
5. What happens institutionally when individuals outwardly commit to being onboard with important initiatives but are inwardly resistant or defensive? What happens when the individuals in question have organizational power or positions of authority?

Scenario 3

The Honeysuckle Havens Museum of Art was a meaningful institution in the life of the community. Honeysuckle Havens was a small town, ensconced in a picturesque setting in the Northeast. It was one of those locales where everyone knew and loved everyone else. Most of all, they valued the museum, not just for its focus on informal learning and aesthetic excellence, but for its site-based welcoming strategies, too. Community members were allowed to use the museum facilities for festivities at a deeply discounted rate. Weddings, birthday parties, and graduation parties were held there regularly. The museum education department held several art competitions throughout the year, encouraging Sunday painters and professional artists alike, and even partnered with the university in the big city to hold a portfolio review every fall for rising seniors. It was truly an extension of everyone's social life.

During the daytime, the museum was bustling with activity; there were always new things to see, even if the staff and volunteers never seemed to change. Some of the docents had been volunteers for decades. One could say that town visitors to the HHMA came just as much to chew the fat as to admire the artwork on view. It was a homogenous community, with very little racial or ethnic diversity, and it was also incredibly conservative. There was still plenty to talk about, though.

The year 2020 was a difficult, bewildering, depressing, and painful year for everyone, because of both the coronavirus and the exhausting resolution of political conflict. Additionally, there were the stay-at-home orders and even sickness among the staff and the community at large. Many staff members had to be furloughed, and of course there were no auxiliary activities to be planned and arranged, so the museum was down to a skeleton crew.

When the staff returned to the museum in the spring of 2021, a management-level employee who was previously known as Larry had undergone a transition and asked to be called Laura. This caused an uproar at the Honeysuckle Havens Museum. Immediately, the gossip mill began to run. How could this happen? Who knew that he was going through this transition? Some were not just outraged, but angry! Why weren't they told or consulted about this possibility? Whatever happened to transparency? Surely the museum director must have known before and should have warned the rest of the staff that a new staff situation was unfolding. After all, everyone on staff and all the volunteers had an opinion about this. Several staff members and docents refused to use the name Laura when referring to their coworker because they said it was against their religious convictions. They also didn't want to see Laura or interact with her: it was simply too upsetting.

Laura knew that there might be some surprise connected with her transition, as there had not been a transgender employee at the museum before, as far as she knew. She was not prepared for her fellow staff members to take her transition so personally. After all, she was exactly the same person—in fact, she was more so: she was her authentic self. She perceived her coworkers' insistence on misgendering her and on using her dead name as acts of hostility and cruelty. She sensed their hesitance to interact with her or desire not to be around her. Laura felt increasingly more isolated at the museum. The friends she thought she had there were now awkward and dismissive. She walked in on a couple of conversations that grew suspiciously silent when those who had been speaking realized she was within earshot. Putting pieces together, she realized that even at the board of directors' level, there was talk about the undue attention Laura was supposedly giving to the museum and how it might affect the bottom line of the institution! Apparently, Laura's transition was a bridge too far for some of the donors at the museum, who had welcomed Laura's presence previously but were now being incredibly intolerant.

Laura approached the director in a private meeting and, in a fit of pique, said she would leave the museum if she was not going to be treated with the dignity and respect she was due. To Laura's horror, the director did not seem to care. The director's only piece of advice was that Laura consider wearing pantsuits and continue to use the men's restroom at the museum if she remained employed.

Please respond to this case study from your own frameworks and under-standing, acknowledging what comes up for you as primary issues of concern or insight.

Additional Questions to Consider

1. At your museum, does it sometimes seem as though it is only the organization itself that is owed respect? Why might that be so?
2. Are there ever conversations about Queer-affirming practices at the museum? Does your museum have policies and official practices that actively prevent discrimination against LGBTQIA+ individuals, and in particular transgender individuals who are increasingly marginalized and in danger?
3. If someone's religion proscribes a certain behavior, such as this case suggests (acknowledging only gender assigned at birth), is a religious person being discriminated against by being asked to refer to transgender individuals by their names? Why or why not?
4. Does your museum have policies about the use of restrooms and restroom facilities that honor the dignity and privacy of staff and visitors?

Scenario 4

Farley, a white museum curator who is nearing retirement age, and whose long and celebrated career has garnered him well-earned praise during his three decades at the Yourtown Museum of History, has become crotchety and spiteful over the last few years. He is especially mean to the newest employees, including a Black curatorial assistant, a visiting scholar from China, and a new office manager whose duties no longer include making coffee in the mornings.

Few people know that Farley has a terminal illness.

The aggrieved staff complains to the director. The curatorial assistant was recently called the "n" word by the curator, and the Chinese employee was mocked for his accent. The director told the staff to grow up and wait the curator's time out until he retires in five years.

Please respond to this case study from your own frameworks and understanding, acknowledging what comes up for you as primary issues of concern or insight.

Additional Questions to Consider

1. When a staff member with significant positional power behaves in ways that mistreat already marginalized and relatively powerless people, how does that impact those individuals and the organization as a whole?

2. Would Farley call his director names to the director's face, or mock the Director's way of speaking? Why or why not?

3. What do each of the individuals in this case need to know about each other to promote greater respect and understanding among themselves?

4. Are some employees exempt from rebuke or censure? Is poor behavior excused because of seniority or circumstance? Who should hold them accountable?

Scenario 5

The hiring manager at Playtime Children's Museum is ready to interview two stellar candidates for a director of education position. Neither of the candidates has prior experience in a museum, but both have related experience, the call for which was new language placed in the job announcements this year in order to place a wider net and be more inclusive.

One of the candidates is an alumna of Gallaudet University and the other graduated from NYU. The hiring manager is not familiar with Gallaudet. When the candidate arrives with an American Sign Language interpreter in tow, the hiring manager becomes visibly flustered and tells the interpreter that there has been a mistake; the position is already filled.

Playtime Children's Museum interviews, accepts, and hires the NYU graduate, who is a great addition to the team, fits right in, and spends many long and enjoyable years at the institution.

Please respond to this case study from your own frameworks and understanding, acknowledging what comes up for you as primary issues of concern or insight.

Additional Questions to Consider

1. What might Playtime Children's Museum have gained by having a deaf employee join the staff?

2. What kind of inclusive hiring practices should there have been to prevent this situation from unfolding the way it did?

3. Do you have a full human resources department at your museum, or is there a small group of senior leaders whose functions include hiring and compensation, workforce compliance, and related functions?

4. Assuming a more robust and concerted effort around DEAI measures, how can you ensure that your anti-discrimination efforts are responsive to the internal and external cultural changes you will be making over time?

5. Are you aware of the five major federal laws and other state regulations and recommendations protecting individuals with disabilities who are interviewing, being hired, currently employed, and leaving your organization? Do you understand your obligations and commitments? Do you realize that disability justice at the museum for staff and visitors is a civil rights imperative?

6. How can you develop more awareness and deepen your understanding of those who are members of various disability communities?

Scenario 6

Marvin is a dedicated museum employee who had worked his way up the organizational ladder over the course of twelve years. He had excelled in his academic pursuits, was one of very few POC in his museum undergraduate and graduate programs, and landed competitive positions in a few museums before settling at the Manypeople Museum of Art and Heritage.

Marvin has never felt that he fit in at the museum. Coworkers and supervisors are polite, but it is clear to him that he's not considered a valued colleague or even a friend. He'll return from a weekend only to find that there was a social gathering to which he and his partner were not invited, while many other museum colleagues in his department were. He is never invited to happy hour and seems to be constantly on the outside of inside jokes.

He does his job impeccably and derives deep satisfaction from his achievements at the museum. His role as associate director of education includes outreach to the larger community, and he is known for creating strong partnerships with schools.

One day Marvin overheard some colleagues discussing salary, and he realizes to his dismay that one of his direct reports, who is white, earns nearly twice as much as he does! Despite receiving stellar annual reviews, Marvin was always told there was no available merit increase. He would occasionally get a small bonus, but his salary remained the same as when he was first hired twelve years before.

When Marvin requests a confidential meeting with the HR director about this discrepancy, he is accused of race baiting, reminded what a singular opportunity he has been given for success, and told not to ask for an increase again.

Please respond to this case study from your own frameworks and understanding, acknowledging what comes up for you as primary issues of concern or insight.

Additional Questions to Consider

1. Can you identify the many instances of assumption and bias that are exemplified in this scenario, in the telling of it, and from Marvin's and his coworkers' perspectives?

2. Many museum leaders discourage their staff from discussing salary among themselves, and some even insinuate that it is illegal or improper to do so. Did you know that there is a decades-old law protecting employees' rights to discuss their salaries with each other?

3. Why might salary transparency be a good thing? How might salary transparency have helped Marvin if it had been revealed in a different way or time in this scenario?

4. Does your organization have clear compensation plans and strategies? Are there consistent and well-documented opportunities to revise compensation packages and rates? Are compensation calculations based on comparative figures across the field, or are they skill based?

5. Why are friendships and positive relationships particularly crucial to the success of minorities in the institution?

Scenario 7

Valerie is the director of development at the Artsy Art Museum. She has just celebrated her twentieth anniversary at the institution. The executive director (ED) surprised her with an anniversary party that was a fancy, festive affair, catered by the museum's upscale restaurant. The ED presented her with a Dom Perignon champagne basket, and her staff had all chipped in to buy her a spa package. Her family and close friends were also in attendance. She introduced them around to people they had heard about but never met in person. It was a lovely and thoughtful two-hour long event in the middle of the workday, and she felt quite cared for. She didn't usually leave work early, but she treated herself to a half day off immediately after the party. Some of her friends helped bring the balloons and gifts to her car.

There have been occasional parties like this over the years. Somehow, the most liked and most personable employees seem to be celebrated, so it's not lost on Valerie that she is considered among the most favored at the Artsy. Other employees who had worked just as long, particularly those who didn't work in front-facing jobs or who worked in positions with less prestige did not get noticed much, but Valerie figured that's what they wanted—to be under the radar—or else they would work in other departments where the impact was greater and they made more of a mark on the institution.

Valerie was glad that she worked in a museum where these kinds of celebrations could happen once in a while. She was glad that her contributions were noticed, because she did work hard, and had raised a lot of money for the museum over the years.

Please respond to this case study from your own frameworks and understanding, acknowledging what comes up for you as primary issues of concern or insight.

Additional Questions to Consider

1. Is there anything amiss in showing appreciation and affection for a job well done, especially when that job entails bringing in significant funds to the museum?

2. Since the development department of a museum is overwhelmingly responsible for the financial stability and health of the organization, shouldn't employees from that department be treated with more honor, respect, and appreciation?

3. What are other ways in which museum employees contribute significantly to a museum's bottom line, reputation, public relations efforts, and goodwill? So many employee contributions go unnoticed, unheralded, and underappreciated.

4. Are there more inclusive and equitable ways in which staff can be celebrated and supported, instead of having public, expensive festivities for some and a lack of acknowledgment for others?

Scenario 8

The Mytown Museum of Modern Art had made an incredibly concerted effort to diversify their staff and volunteer corps over the past five years. They believed they were far ahead of the curve, having added an accounts coordinator of color and a museum educator who was blind among their eight new hires.

The next phase in their inclusion strategy was to cultivate members and potential donors of color. A friend-raising event was planned jointly by the Membership and Development Departments. True to their understanding of best practice, they had the event underwritten by donors, and the music and catered food were culturally relevant. After several months of intentional efforts, they developed a sizable contact list, established some new relationships, and ultimately received more than one thousand yeses on their RSVP list. Success!

The big evening finally came. During afterhours, when the museum was closed to the public, it came alive. First was the cocktail hour in the great hall, with its stately marble floors and massive columns. There were delectable hors d'oeuvres prepared by a local soul food restaurant instead of by the museum's regular caterer, passed around on elegant trays by wait staff; cocktails and beverages flowing and made to order at an open bar; and animated conversations sparking the air. The museum director and chief curator made welcoming remarks. This evening would mark a new emphasis on new friends in the BIPOC community and in particular the Black community in the city.

The main event that evening was a panel discussion and musical performance by a well-known public speaker and a chanteuse. As guests made their way to the art galleries and to the auditorium, they noticed several uniformed security guards and armed city policemen stationed just inside both venues, as well as patrolling connecting passageways.

The presence of these officers elicited reactions of confusion, incredulity, anger, and betrayal. Why had the museum done this? What was the message it was trying to send? Did they not trust their new friends, who were hopefully to become regular visitors and supporters of the museum?

Some guests responded viscerally, with physiological reactions to the phenomenon of being unduly policed and monitored. One woman was heard asking for someone to get her inhaler out of her purse and to get her to the nearest exit for fresh air. A few angry men shouted and cursed. It was a large crowd, to be certain, but more importantly there was a disconnect between the idea of a relaxing and welcoming fete at the museum, tailored to new friends, and the heavily guarded event they had been subjected to.

Many guests ended up leaving well before the night's formal entertainment transpired. "I'm supposed to feel welcome here?" a young woman was overheard to ask sarcastically.

By the following Monday, a small group of staff of color had heard about the increased security and police presence at the event. They asked to speak with the director and were immediately given his undivided attention.

"Listen," he said, "It was all just a mammoth misunderstanding. People were just getting out of whack over nothing. There's a rule on the books that states . . . ." He reached behind him for a large, heavy binder, swung it over to the conference table and read from one paragraph among hundreds in the thick ringed sheaf, "Yes; here it is—if there are more than 999 adult visitors in any of the museum buildings at the same time, this is the correct ratio of security to bodies. And yes, the city police must assist if there are over 1,000 people. City rules." He closed the binder and smiled. "End of story."

"No," said Anitra. "This can't be right. Are you taking into consideration the optics of the situation? Also the feelings and very real threats faced by your audience?"

"Are you raising your voice to me?" asked the director angrily. "Please watch your tone. Also, four years ago, when we had a big panel discussion here, we had the same number of security guards and policemen here."

"But that was attended by all white people!" shouted Cedric. "Please tell me you see the difference!"

"I actually don't," said the director, shaking his head. "I'm sorry, but I think you people just want to see the worst in everything. This is all for everyone's protection. Do you know how much money was spent on additional security?"

Please respond to this case study from your own frameworks and understanding, acknowledging what comes up for you as primary issues of concern or insight.

Additional Questions to Consider
1. How important is cultural awareness when one is attempting to authentically engage and bridge differences?
2. What is the difference between managing risk to property and risking the loss of relationships?
3. With all the planning that must have occurred, do you think there was dialogue around the impact of having a heavy security presence at an event where there would be a majority of Black people at a

predominantly white institutional building? Who would dialogue about this matter?

4. Might it have been important to include people of color in planning for an event that was intended to cultivate people of color?

5. How could the regulations about the ratio of security guards to people been upheld without seeming overwhelming or threatening to those particular guests that night?

6. If you were the director or the head of physical facilities overseeing security staff, how would you handle a future situation with similar demographics or circumstances?

Scenario 9

The Board of Trustees at the Lovely Museum of Beautiful Things was an incredibly generous, hardworking body. The museum was a venerable, longstanding institution that had a reputation of excellence in the field.

That said, like many museums in the United States as evaluated and reported in the late 2010s, most of the executive leadership and board members of the Lovely Museum of Beautiful Things were white, cisgender, heterosexual men. There was not a lot of ethnic, racial, national, or gender diversity among them, and that needed to change. There was very little economic diversity. Most of the board members believed their responsibility to be entirely fiduciary. They each donated more than the recommended $50,000 annually to support the museum. Those who could donate substantially more did, and did so with gusto. Those who could contribute in other ways donated time and talent in addition to their treasure. They enjoyed the camaraderie and association they shared as board members and strongly felt their duty of care and weight of responsibility to the professional community.

As their museum joined many others in the field that were examining their commitment to diversity, equity, accessibility, and inclusion, the board of trustees was glad to have new tools and benchmarks by which to gauge their responsibilities and progress. They were certainly aware of their relative homogeneity, which they attributed to the field at large and a perceived disinterest among other community members toward museum matters. They formed a subcommittee to cultivate five new board members out of a possible eight available spots. They hoped to find at least one individual for each spot who was a person of color, identified as female, was from the queer community, had a visible disability, or had an annual income of less than the contributing amount (and who would, of course, not be asked to donate monetarily as part of their board duties).

The museum leadership and staff had independently, but with the board's blessing, welcomed a new staff member who would lead initial efforts to assess and engage the museum in baseline training. This staff member felt very strongly about including the board, and about sharing a philosophy that involved transforming the organizational culture, rethinking leadership, and rooting the work of DEAI in racial justice and anti-oppression. This would mean that each individual would commit to working on their biases and prejudices as a first step.

The new DEAI leader had a meeting with the board of trustees that did not go well at all. The board members were profoundly offended that anyone would imagine they needed to work on their own biases—as if they had any! After all, they had independently come up with a list of five identity markers for filling board seats, and cumulatively they had agreed to pay one of the new trustees' dues. After all the board did for the museum, how insulting for a new employee to think so little of them!

The board of the Lovely Museum of Beautiful Things refused to cooperate with the workshops, dialogues, benchmarking, and training as experienced by the rest of the staff, insisting they had no time to give despite their interest. Behind closed doors, and in the privacy of their text messages and phone calls to each other, they excoriated the staff member's process and called into question the museum's judgment.

Please respond to this case study from your own frameworks and understanding, acknowledging what comes up for you as primary issues of concern or insight.

Additional Questions to Consider

1. How can museum boards be reconfigured mentally as servant leaders instead of solely governors?

    Note: Servant leadership, a term coined by Robert Greenleaf in the 1970s, describes an approach used by those with positional power that centers people across the institution and their developmental needs: emphasizing self-awareness, valuing contributions, modeling empathy and compassion; welcoming collaboration, fostering healing, and engaging community. A servant leader prioritizes relationships over measurable results; and considers a successful project to be one in which the team moves toward the goal in an environment where contributors are cared for, welcomed, respected, heard, and engaged.

2. How can staff and boards connect more meaningfully?

3. What are some cultural impediments that may prevent boards from relating or collaborating with museum leaders and staff when appropriate?

Scenario 10

Jin was deeply affected by recent spates of physical violence against Asian Americans, spurred on by political rhetoric about the supposed origins of the coronavirus. He had lived in his neighborhood for most of his adult life; it was a quiet part of the city, in a diversely populated area filled with folks of various ethnicities, interests, and walks of life. His neighborhood bordered five or six academic institutions, including the university museum, where he worked part-time.

Jin was known for being quiet and almost a loner. It wasn't true, though—he was just contemplative, and it was common for those in his family and maybe for others of Korean and Chinese upbringing to listen first, then speak when there was something important to share.

After this rash of violence, Jin wanted to talk more with his coworkers, and he was glad when they engaged him. Even though he had worked for the museum for a few years, the nature of the institutions—both the university and the museum—was such that he felt he was getting to know people all over again. As his white colleagues and colleagues of color were reintroducing themselves, he noticed that they were being particularly complimentary in odd ways. It didn't take him long to understand that they were wrongly attributing characteristics to him that he did not possess, because of bias and attribution stereotypes about Asians. He also suspected he was being mistaken for someone else (who didn't even look like him).

Jin's well of anger bubbled over, and he found himself loudly and firmly stating: "I am not Jun; I'm Jin! I do not fix computers. I do not even

Your New Boss
Copyright 2020 Sam Day. Used with permission, created for Cecile Shellman Consulting

know how. I'm not good at math; I'm the museum attendant and I often assist the curator with condition checks and loans. Please stop telling me I speak good English; I was born in Columbus like most of you. Also, I don't know of any good Thai restaurants."

He turned and walked right back out of the building, calling his supervisor from his cell phone to request a personal day off.

As he was leaving, he heard some people still in the room laughing and saying, "Wow. That overly emotional Japanese guy, huh? We've been really nice to him. Asians are great. At least we're not treating him like those guys we saw on TV beating up those elderly people."

Please respond to this case study from your own frameworks and situations, acknowledging what comes up for you as primary issues of concern or insight.

Additional Questions to Consider

1. Do you know the myth of the Model Minority and why it is problematic? How does this play out in museums? How is it demonstrated in this scenario?

2. Many Asian Americans encounter the *perpetual foreigner* stereotype, which is expressed in micro aggressions that target the notion that Asian Americans cannot possibly be generationally or naturalized Americans, and must be from "somewhere else," and an *exotic other*. How can this stereotype be damaging?

It Takes More Than a Token Effort
Copyright 2020 Sam Day. Used with permission, created for Cecile Shellman Consulting

CHAPTER SIX

~

Our Duty to the Field
and Each Other

Cultural Change Must Precede Change in Policy and Practice—
Unless change happens from the inside, we cannot expect authentic
organizational change or external results

What were we waiting for?

Back in August 2014, when eighteen-year old Michael Brown of Ferguson, Missouri, was shot and killed by police officer Darren Wilson after a scuffle ostensibly over the teenager's walking in the street instead of on the sidewalk, the nation's conscience was piqued and horrified by the excessive brutality by law enforcement toward Black bodies.

For weeks, crowds in Ferguson and elsewhere protested in anguish and fury, tired, troubled, and traumatized that yet another Black life had been senselessly, violently, taken.

The then-newish movement called Black Lives Matter powerfully modeled the principle that unjust killings were wrong not just because it's illegal and unfair, but because the people, communities, and individuals whose lives are taken matter. These felled bodies, once full of vigor and life, had had love in their lives: passions, dreams, histories, heritage, families, and for some, even progeny. Sadly, they also had a harrowing legacy of minimization, brutality, and atrocity at the hands of the systems that killed them. Without this acknowledgment and recognition, the murder of Michael Brown, and those of a myriad other people of color, by law enforcers are unique tragedies perpetuated by hateful individuals. Adherents to the Black Lives Matter creed marched in the streets, made protest signs, and challenged those who didn't believe Black people truly mattered to look inwardly and question why.

To decry police brutality is not to focus solely on the police; there are individual peace officers who are kind, decent individuals motivated by career aspirations and a love of their fellow humans. The police system is simply broken; so are the many systems that control and set the narratives about the supposed superiority and right to dominate of the majority in America. Whether subtly or in terrifying determined forthrightness, the idea that there are ruling classes, ethnicities, genders, or nationalities who are entitled to power and exempt from consequence prevails with dismaying obduracy.

Museums are among other fields, institutions, and enterprises that have counted on the continuation of white leadership, tradition, collections, prestige, finance, visibility—often at the expense and to the detriment of people of color, people with economic need, and others at the margins.

In September 2014, University of Pittsburgh School of Law faculty member David Harris—a leading scholar and lecturer in criminal justice reform—spoke to a standing-room-only audience as part of the programming for the Carnegie Museum of Natural History's presentation of *Race: Are We So Different?*, an exhibition developed by the Science Museum of Minnesota devoted to examining the history of America's system of race and the implications of racism on individuals and society. Mr. Harris began his riveting talk with the assertion that the genesis of policing in this country was slave patrols: that these were the first policing units, meant to round up and brutally punish recalcitrant enslaved persons. The lecture was accompanied by chilling black-and-white visuals, photographs of menacing policemen turning hoses, guns, or Tasers on protesting crowds. Seen side by side, these images were barely indistinguishable by date.

Changes must happen in order for change to occur. We must be the change we seek.

The programming for *Race: Are We So different?* augmented the themes discussed in the exhibition, and certainly the themes of police brutality, racial profiling, and the school-to-prison pipeline were germane to the museum's display. There was no question that this particular lecture connected to the material and also resonated with audiences of color, whose patronage the museum was trying to assure.

That said, this informative lecture, the classical Indian dance performance in the majestic Carnegie Museum of Art Hall of Architecture, the spoken word night in the galleries, the poetry workshop, and scores of other programs for adults and children were all programmatic add-ons rather than fully incorporated outgrowths of a value-driven DEAI approach. Though popular and well presented, few, if any, of these programs were attended by the museum's leadership or considered to be part of the organizational ethos. It was wholly transactional: even though there was a no-cost or low-cost model of admission to these events to ensure a wide audience, the events were still related to the exhibition itself, rather than answering the call to a system-wide strategy for equity and inclusion.

The Marketing and Communications Department had been given the autonomy to create programming, advertorials, and other ancillary happenings to respond creatively to the exhibition. The brilliant interim director was eager to make inroads and forge partnerships with many small businesses headed by entrepreneurs of color—businesses that were elated to hear from and work with the museum.

It was a magical seven months. In an effort to drive attendance to the exhibition, I had been hired as a marcom specialist exclusively to develop the partnerships, public relations, and programming that would connect with the audiences of color we were attempting to reach, and who had not frequented the museum to the desired degree. Collaborating with staff from the Education Department who typically designed and coordinated museum activities for visitors, we employed marketing strategies and found unique ways to draw audiences to the blockbuster exhibition: everything from placing a kiosk with free copies of the award-winning weekly local African American newspaper the *New Pittsburgh Courier* on the exhibit floor for visitors to take, to numerous television and radio features touting the exhibition as an educational tool and must-see intercultural experience, to giving personalized guided tours on request.

The success of the exhibition in its ability to connect with the local and regional Black community and others who were eager to learn about and discuss racism and social injustice was not lost on members of the museum's administration. A month later I would be offered the position of diversity catalyst, the first chief diversity officer role at Carnegie Institute, intended to be at the helm of an initiative of diversity, equity, access, and inclusion at the four museums under the Carnegie banner.

In 2014, very few museums had roles that focused on DEAI, and leaders in the field were seemingly at odds regarding the purpose or efficacy of a museum DEAI officer role. For some the position was supposed to reside in the human resources office, as a specialist to advise on hiring ethnically and racially diverse employees. Other museum thought leaders imagined more robust interpretations of the role but knew that a single position could not effectively manage it. It soon became very clear that within the museum itself, as well as within the local, regional, and national museum communities, there was little consensus about what a DEAI strategy could realistically entail.

It was also clear that few practitioners in the museum connected the idea of social justice work with a DEAI approach. In fact, some were very adamant that museums were neutral places, and neither employees nor visitors should consider the premises a place for gathering, strategizing, conspiring, or dismantling oppression where it resided. Still, museum employees walked around with worried faces and wiped away tears in hallways, even as others rolled their eyes or dared to say: "We need to wait for the reports to see what Michael Brown actually did when the cameras weren't rolling." So many museum staffers in various museums across the country desired to make statements decrying the needless killing of Black people by police, but museums as institutions were quiet. Corporations spoke out. Individuals marched. Museums did not.

I do remember making phone calls to museum colleagues across the country, asking what their museums were planning to do, if their CEOs and board chairs had okayed a public statement. Some of them hemmed and hawed. Others cited institutional policy against making political statements.

It took the African American Association of Museums (AAAM) to make a bold, groundbreaking, heartbreaking rebuke of the violence toward black men and women at the hands of those sworn to serve and protect. This missive served as permission for other museum associations and individual museums to follow suit. Once AAAM came through with a message, a smattering of museum organizations and collectives penned their own letters of support.

It was nothing like what we saw in June 2020, however. I don't know too many museums now that aren't pledging their support for anti-racist efforts. Some of these stirring promises have brought tears to my eyes. Many of these were by organizations that have few, if any, Black employees or board members.

The year 2014 and those immediately following also saw the beginning of social media campaigns such as #MuseumsRespondToFerguson and #MuseumsAreNotNeutral. By 2017 the American Alliance of Museums had substantially increased the number of workshops, presentations, and panels that tackled DEAI concerns.

Yet there is still hesitancy on the part of many museums to fully stand behind the concept of DEAI as a cultural reform and reconciliation proposition.

Systemic racism is not just about the death of nonwhite bodies at the hands of people who champion ideals that support white people in power. It's also about the death of dreams of those who are not white: the removal of hope, economic power, access to resources, and pride in accomplishment.

Fighting against systemic racism in the museum world is about battling those urges to retain objects that had been pillaged from lands and communities that had been colonized and subjugated. It might mean questioning and changing the unspoken model of personal wealth, family legacy, or prestige being qualifications for board service, donor suitability, or desired museum visitor traits—especially when those biases exclude people of color. Systemic racism in museums might look like certain hallowed traditions that are biases in disguise. Interrupting and dismantling racism at the systemic level will mean questioning the practice of collecting: not just what is collected and displayed, but by whom, and for whom. Who benefits most from these acquisitions? Who is aggrandized or made more powerful? Whose status is buttressed?

Whenever museum leaders say they are timid about following through on DEAI challenges, I remind them of their impassioned, anguished faces in the late spring of 2020 when they invoked the name of George Floyd and wondered what they could do to help. What can they do to help? This. This is what you do.

On August 28, 1963, in the shadow of the Lincoln Memorial, Dr. Martin Luther King Jr. spoke about an uncashed check that America had yet to honor. In the same speech that famously talked about his four children holding hands with children of other races, he firmly chastised the promisors of freedom and equity, accusing them of false promises, saying the bounced check was in fact stamped with the response "Insufficient funds."

The payment of this check is not in the form of discrete and occasional acts of benevolence. Rather, it's a sacred guarantee that life, liberty, and the pursuit of happiness are equally available to people who have been denied these rights for too long.

To connect these promises to the responsibilities of inclusive hiring, culturally competent collections care, and sensitivity training—all important parts of the whole, but not the whole by any means—we must accept that this is a call to a complete and utter cultural change. Each museum must look within to see how their current practices unwittingly or intentionally support systemic injustice. We must each look internally to see how we as individuals perpetuate injustice by looking the other way, not speaking up, or not continually working to dismantle it. As colleagues, we must be brave enough to continue the mission, even when naysayers disparage the process or attempt to derail it.

Cultural change precipitates policy change. Museums can create statements on reams of paper that remain untouched and unseen by those who smilingly swear to enact them. Museum leaders can couch their plans in flowery language delivered before cameras and microphones and yet say nothing. Until and unless the entire museum family commits to working together to achieving DEAI goals, the process of cultural change will fail.

I think back to my days at the John F. Kennedy Presidential Library and Museum: What made those days so special? I'm convinced that the leaders saw themselves as allies, coconspirators, and change agents along with the staff. The culture, under inspired leadership and in a spirit of trust and camaraderie, was one of shared purpose, community service, and team building. While no internal work culture is perfect, in my memory the environment at the John F. Kennedy Presidential Library and Museum was quite close. Colleagues had genuine mutual affection for one another, and we all believed we were engaged in a noble cause that was far greater than writing educational materials or organizing programmatic events. We talked about social justice as a matter of course. Our exhibitions, which were already replete with great oratory about aspirations of unity, were used to address internal and community-wide calls to civic action. Our community-outreach efforts were neither gimmicks nor slick marketing strategies. If we saw or heard of a laudable deed in the community, especially one accomplished by a hero who would otherwise have gone unsung, we created a special day to celebrate them, bestowing a Make a Difference Award on them in the company of their families and friends. This became an annual event.

I envision the same for museums across the country: humble and dedicated leaders who practice what they teach laboring alongside staff at all levels of museum service, using exhibition programs and exhibitions to teach about and challenge us to confront oppression. Museums should be ready and willing to confront those challenges within our own practices also, holding a mirror to ourselves.

Servant leaders are inspired to change themselves, each other, and the world.

Culturally proficient people acknowledge the need to change themselves and patiently work with colleagues to bring them along in the process. Those with privilege understand their responsibility to let other voices be lifted and valued. Culturally proficient people are teachable and continuously learning, improving their practice daily.

As culture keeps a steady center, the business of museum skills and strategies must still be tended.

Following are some steps you may choose to consider when mapping your course to a holistic approach.

Creating Your Diversity, Equity, Access, and Inclusion Strategy

Your DEAI process is part of your internal cultural change rather than a separate program that occasionally addresses working parts of the whole. I am often asked by museum practitioners to simply give them a list of resources to read and watch, accompanied by a checklist of the changes that need to be made to each departmental area. I don't believe that is helpful or even possible because each organization must address the values, culture, and DEAI concerns at the center before seeing how they radiate to every aspect of their museum life and work. No two museums will have exactly the problems, barriers, and limitations experienced equally by their marginalized constituents. Some museums may need to concentrate on becoming more socially and civically aware, whether or not they have the ability to focus on building staff diversity or improving their work climate. Others are ready to have their museum art classes draw picket signs to protest injustice. Yet others are struggling to convince staff members to treat each other kindly.

Ultimately, the goal is social justice and rooting out oppression where it exists. Focusing on checklists or steps to increase "diversity numbers" and becoming disappointed when it doesn't happen after a brief predetermined time—usually an unrealistic goal—is missing the point.

I liken it to a cake that a group of friends is invited to eat. Instead of waiting until it leaves the oven, the group crowds around the baker, and each begins consuming singular ingredients, wondering why the cake tastes so funny.

An Entire Approach: Organizational Change

With shared values or core cultural beliefs in the center, you can begin to envision a workplace climate, museum ethic, set of inclusive practices, and welcoming approach that suit your museum.

Strategy

- Diversity: Include partners, staff, and collaborators from various identity groups and communities in strategic planning and implementation; bring them onto the staff, and compensate them appropriately. Consider all the many and varied ways that your museum can benefit from the wisdom of all your constituents and valued partners.
- Equity: Strategy visioning and implementation should include expanding opportunities for external constituents, clients, and applicants and investing more financial resources in their growth and development as well as their meritorious achievements. As you engage in planning, invite, welcome, and listen to all participants,

It's Not a Cake Until You Mix it
Copyright 2020 Sam Day. Used with permission, created for Cecile Shellman Consulting

taking care to recognize those who might not previously have had opportunities to share in executive or managerial meetings. Do you utilize a variety of methods to circulate and solicit information? Does everyone have the time they need to adequately read, ponder, respond, and react to prompts requiring feedback?

- Accessibility: Strive for transparency to the degree that it is possible and prudent. Reexamine traditions and norms that privilege few and prevent them from sharing or ceding power and responsibility that could be borne by willing and able workers. Accept staff, volunteers, visitors, and community members exactly as they are. Value your staff for who they are, not their job titles or credentials.

- Inclusion: Seek input from the internal and external individuals and communities who will be most affected by the changes you plan to implement. Take time, and be intentional about selecting individuals from inside and outside the museum to form focus groups, advisory panels, and convenings to obtain feedback and to begin engaging in meaningful relationships with the museum.

Structure

- In governance, administration, management, programming, and every other level of the internal organization, actively recruit, cultivate, hire, and appoint a diversity/representation of BIPOC and others who have traditionally been marginalized.

- Create pathways for those who are typically least represented to hold increasingly more agency and power in the organization. Understand that keeping BIPOC workers in positions that are low paying or offer no chance of ascending the organization ladder is also oppression.

- Clearly communicate the organizational structure, both internally and externally. Does everyone on staff understand who is responsible for ultimately making decisions and influencing others? Is there clear access to those with decision-making power? Strive for less of an atmosphere of secrecy or mystery and more of an open, engaging space.

- Solicit, receive, and seek to value input about other cultural ideas of effective organizational structures. Do not threaten or punish those who have divergent views or suggest improvements.

Systems

What are the daily activities and projects that get the museum work done? What is the essential business of the museum? How are those activities accomplished? Is there strict oversight or a more autonomous style of handling matters? How quickly are problems solved, and how do new projects get off the ground? Who are the leaders, influencers, and closers? Are they the same people who hold the formal titles?

Use a DEAI lens for all of these. How will you ensure diversity, equity, access, and inclusion in:

- Collections care and management
  - What are some practical and ethical concerns in current collections-care practice? Do your curators, registrars, acquisitions committee, and others belong to professional associations, organizations, and committees that discuss best practices in navigating these matters? Is your museum actively working to repatriate objects that were wrongfully acquired and do not belong in a collection? Do you have as a value the uplifting of marginalized people through the collecting, care, and preserving of their material culture with their input and consent?
  - Do you know who created each object in your collection and how they prefer to be named and memorialized? How often do you review and revise your accessions records to reflect new understandings and practices that affirm non-dominant-culture artists and object makers?
- Curating
  - Which objects, and whose stories, are being collected and told? Do you currently have a practice of co-curating exhibitions with the ethnically and racially diverse communities whose work you display or plan to exhibit at a later time? Do you value and welcome the work of other excluded minorities such as members of the queer community and people who have disabilities? Do you make a conscious effort not to favor individuals and communities who are typically and traditionally heralded?
- Exhibition development

- ◦ Are your exhibition themes educational, enriching, and culturally responsive? Do they connect with themes and subjects that are meaningful and present? Do your curators, interns, and researchers work in secret and solitude, or do they value other staff and outside community members as subject-matter experts and artists in their own right?
- ◦ Do you plan multiple exhibitions simultaneously? Scaffolding exhibition plans can be an effective way to work collaboratively and efficiently. A phased-exhibition-plan approach can make best use of museum workers' time, frontloading big-picture thinking, and allowing team members to strategize, evaluate, and work conceptually with exhibit elements long before fabricating them. As one exhibition plan nears fruition and another is just being approved for further development, junior and senior team members can exchange roles, be mentored or share wisdom when necessary, and take advantage of converging processes. For example, standard accoutrements such as exhibit labels could be designed and made at the same time for several exhibitions once the object lists are confirmed.
- • Exhibition design and build
  - ◦ As you design the conceptual and actual spaces that the exhibition galleries comprise, are you mindful of the various bodies, minds, and abilities that will temporarily inhabit those pathways? Do you study, understand, and apply the laws and regulations pertaining to universal design and accommodations for people with disabilities? Do you communicate the importance of following ADAAG (Americans With Disabilities Act Accessibility Guidelines) standards to preparators and construction teams who may only be familiar with building codes, and who may be tempted to be imprecise with measurements?
- • Museum Education and Interpretation
  - ◦ Do you lead school groups and adult tour groups from all walks of life through the museum, or are there preferred groups whose patronage you solicit and welcome over others? Do you make judgments or assumptions about groups from certain communities

or neighborhoods and their capacity to comprehend, enjoy, or appreciate art, history, or science?

- ○ Are your interpretive materials written and recorded at various levels? Do you employ best practices of accommodation for people with disabilities?
- ○ Are your programs developed for various audiences, interests, and cultures? As you create them, are you engaging in dialogue and conversation with individuals from the communities you intend to serve, especially if the messages are about those communities?
- ○ Do your educators, docents, and volunteers represent diverse ethnic, racial, gender identity, age, and sexual orientation backgrounds?
- • Visitor Services
  - ○ Do you make a conscious effort to use welcoming, inclusive language when interacting with each other and with the public? It's important to avoid making assumptions about individuals in groups and how they are related. Do you meet often to engage in training and helpful workshop exercises to increase your awareness and improve your practice? Do you work independently and together to examine your biases and find ways to mitigate them?

Governance

Instead of having strict mandatory (and often steep) donation requirements at the trustee level, perhaps board members could be invited to give of their time, treasure, or talent—each equally considered viable supports of the institution. Board members, like everyone else, need to dig deep and look closely at their own biases and their levels of cultural competence, improving what they see to be insufficient for the new focus on social justice.

Development and Membership

Membership as a practice can almost be seen as antithetical to the idea of inclusion. Shouldn't we all be members? I challenge membership and development professionals to think of, and create, models that are increasingly less exclusionary and more about exchanging value.

Staffing

- Recruiting:

Continue to develop and improve your internal work culture as you actively recruit new hires, no matter how senior or junior the position. If you are going to tout your commitment to diversity, equity, accessibility, and inclusion and yet maintain a stressful or contentious work environment, how welcoming are you truly being when you seek unsuspecting talent?

- Hiring:

Without realizing it, many museums seek to hire for diversity, yet employ for sameness. Are you truly interested in the various viewpoints and cultural richness that people from diverse backgrounds can provide, or is the push for numeric diversity just that: numeric?

   ○ Make sure that your hiring practices are as free from bias as possible. Treat each applicant and interviewee the same. If one candidate is being interviewed over lunch at a nice restaurant, you should interview all others in the same restaurant and for the same amount of time. Be careful of the kinds of questions you ask. Some standard, traditional questions you might have used in the past or have heard about are not really necessary for all job-seeking prospects or processes, yet they are still used. Do certain positions really need to be filled by those with advanced degrees? Why or why not? Is there a reason you must know about their immediate past compensation or their salary history? Some professionals find themselves in extenuating situations where they need to accept employment at salaries below their preference or need. One's salary does not reflect one's worth or ability as a human being.

   ○ Work on auditing, examining, and redefining practices and policies that are focused on dominant-culture ideals and might disfavor or disenfranchise other staff who are not accustomed or suited to these ways of working or behaving.

Style

- What is the work culture like? How are your current staff, board members, and other constituents experiencing your internal work culture? Might it help to conduct a survey or climate study to yield responses? When you administer the survey and receive results, it's important not to be defensive about what the data reveals. Data is best used as diagnostics. Once we have information, we can act to improve.

- We need to live what we learn and practice what is preached. It's not enough to train our professionals to incorporate DEAI principles in their technical work when our daily work environment is fraught.
- Consider setting aside specific venues—virtual and actual—for people to reflect, commiserate, speak candidly, and think quietly about matters pertaining to social justice while at work. We are asking employees to think and behave in emotional ways to a degree they might not have done previously. Some may need actual spaces to emote and unwind. The emotional toll on our collective is real.
- Foster an environment of trust in the workplace. Reduce the level of competition among peers. Treat one another with dignity and respect.

Skills
Focus on developing the following skills, both as a group and individually:

- Emotional intelligence
- Bias reduction (including new ways of interviewing and conducting grant review panels)
- Inclusive language and other cross-cultural communication skills
- Participating in courageous conversation/dialoguing about topics that may be seen as difficult or uncomfortable, but are necessary to share information that can be helpful to understand cultural contexts and current events
- Resiliency
- Patience
- Analysis of power: Whom does your strategy or values help or harm?
- Committing to do the least harm and to support those who are typically marginalized

Now That You Know What to Do, How Do You Do It?

Start out by creating a museum value statement about DEAI. This statement is different from your existing DEAI message. It is not a list of activities, programs, or commitments that you intend to make to communities in crisis. Your DEAI value statement is a rationale for why your entire museum should be involved in this work. This should be an internal document that is honest, incisive, specific, and not intended for the public. Once you have created this statement in collaboration with your staff, board members, and volunteers, you will have a shared ethic from which to design your work going forward.

In order to engage in this process, you will need to:

1. Gauge the level of trust and interest laterally and vertically across the institution. If you administer a survey, you might receive frank and authentic responses that will help you understand why some may have reservations about your intended DEAI approach.

2. Consider your reputation among the internal and external communities with which you interact. Are there communities you have hurt in the past, or who mistrust you? Be candid when you state the rationale for engaging in a DEAI initiative.

3. Be as transparent and collaborative as possible. For large museums, the creation of your value statement can happen with the input of a DEAI task force or committee that is representative of your whole staff.

4. What should your statement include? Who are you in relation to your staff, board, and local communities? Be honest about the organization's own oppressive or harmful practices that you wish to revise.

5. Think of your museum as a powerful entity that benefits some communities and individuals and marginalizes others. Consider hierarchies, power differentials, privilege, majority culture visibility, and assumptions of authority. Who benefits most from working at the museum? Who is marginalized or benefits least? Who has the ability to advance, participate, and have access? Name and accept these groups or individuals, and use the statement to commit to changing your traditions.

6. Consider your existing museum audiences: How are they typically involved in ways that are not transactional? What are barriers to their full inclusion?

7. Regarding your views about systemic oppression, what is your organization's commitment to the work of social justice? "We value social inclusion" is meaningless. Use explicit, specific language. Consider saying, "We see the ways in which marginalized communities are ignored and less valued in our museum community, and we have been culpable in perpetuating this inequity." Accept and declare responsibility where applicable.

8. Share the document with staff, board members, volunteers, and others. Request input by way of in-person meetings, electronic means, and long-form writing.

9. Consider realistic solutions to challenges. What is your internal capacity? What is your external capacity? Attach measurable goals to your activities that align with your DEAI strategy. Who in the museum has the power, skill, and will to initiate this plan and follow through? Are you inviting and accepting the marginalized audiences you seek to attract? Do they have meaningful long-term impacts? Listen to their concerns. Don't be overly worried about who is right as much as what is right. Challenge your assumptions.

10. After writing your aspirational purpose statement, compare it against any existing collateral that you might currently share internally or externally, such as your EEO statement, public relations material, marketing communication statements, or job announcements. Are the messages the same? How consistent are they? Are you overstating your intent in the front-facing materials? Do they read as authentic?

Now comes the hard work, and the work that only your institution can do. Fully transparent, and authentic in your humility, you are ready to rebuild, boldly asserting your ultimate goal and working to support each other in moving forward.

It will take longer than you think. It will be more painful than you think. But you are stronger than you think, and it will be worth it.

~

Appendix

Additional Readings and Resources

Books

Betsch Cole, Johnnetta, and Laura L. Lott (ed.). *Diversity, Equity, Accessibility, and Inclusion in Museums* (2019).

Gokcigdem, Elif M. (ed.). *Fostering Empathy Through Museums* (2016).

Hollins, Caprice, and Ilsa Govan. *Diversity, Equity, and Inclusion: Strategies for Facilitating Conversations on Race* (2015).

Ross, Howard J. *Everyday Bias: Identifying and Navigating Unconscious Judgments in Our Daily Lives,* (2020).

Sandell, Richard, and Eithne Nightingale (ed.). *Museums, Equality, and Social Justice* (2012).

Williams, Bari A. *Diversity in the Workplace: Eye-Opening Interviews to Jumpstart Conversations about Identity, Privilege, and Bias* (2020).

Web Articles and Websites

American Alliance of Museums, Definitions of Diversity, Equity, Accessibility, and Inclusion, https://www.aam-us.org/programs/diversity-equity-accessibility-and-inclusion/facing-change-definitions/. April 30, 2018.

Refocusing Museums on People: My Dreams for Museums in a Post-COVID World, Mike Murawski, https://artmuseumteaching.com/2021/04/26/refocusing-museums-on-people/. April 23, 2021.

Cecile Shellman Consulting Blog, http://www.cecileshellmanconsulting.com /blog

The Incluseum Blog, https://incluseum.com/

MASS Action, https://www.museumaction.org/

Speak Out Now, https://www.speakoutnow.org

Index

~

About the Author

Cecile Shellman is a fulltime consultant in diversity, equity, accessibility, and inclusion for museums. From 2014 to 2018, she worked for Carnegie Museums of Pittsburgh as their diversity catalyst—a first-of-its-kind position on their senior executive staff, heading DEAI initiatives for the Carnegie Museum of Art, Carnegie Museum of Natural History, Carnegie Science Center, and Andy Warhol Museum. She was the only African American on that institution's Institute Leadership Team, which included museum directors, institute vice presidents, and the chief executive officer. She specialized in group diversity and inclusion training, leadership counseling, public speaking, and workshop facilitation.

Cecile understands museums, having a long and varied history working in a variety of departments in museums from the early 1990s to the present day, from the intermountain West to New England, New York, and Appalachia. Her past appointments have included education curator, exhibit curator, director of education, group and community outreach specialist, artistic director for visual arts and exhibitions, and the Culturally Responsive Arts Education Program manager at Pittsburgh Public Schools, connecting students to museums and other cultural assets.

Ms. Shellman has long served in leadership positions for the American Alliance of Museums (AAM), and is immediate past chair of their Professional Network's Diversity Committee, DIVCOM. She is a frequent presenter at the AAM Annual Convening on topics related to DEAI, has been featured and published in *MUSEUM* magazine and on AAM's website, and was a contributor to Johnnetta Betsch Cole and Laura L. Lott (eds.), *Diversity, Equity, Accessibility, and Inclusion in Museums* (2019).

Cecile Shellman Consulting's current and past clients for diversity, equity, accessibility, and inclusion work include the Philadelphia Museum of Art, Utah Museums Association, Association of Museum Curators, Westmoreland Museum of American Art, The Eric Carle Museum of Picture Book Art, Discovery Place, The Bruce Museum of Arts and Science, The Children's Museum of Pittsburgh, John F. Kennedy Presidential Library and Museum, San Francisco Museum of Modern Art, Frick Art and Historical Center in Pittsburgh, Palo Alto Art Center, Palo Alto Junior Museum and Zoo, August Wilson African American Cultural Center, and Greater Pittsburgh Arts Council. In 2019 she was named one of ten Senior Diversity Fellows for DEAI at the American Alliance of Museums. This active assignment pairs its expert fellows with museums across the country to train their boards and executive leadership, with the goal of diversifying the leadership exponentially over time. Cecile's assigned city is Chicago, where her client museums include the Intuit Museum, the Aurora Fire Museum, and the Chicago History Center. She is also a qualified administrator (QA) for the Intercultural Development Inventory, considered the premier assessment for gauging cultural capacity.